Helping Kids Help

ORGANIZING SUCCESSFUL CHARITABLE PROJECTS

Renée Heiss

Skyhorse Publishing, Inc.

Skyhorse Publishing books may be purchased in bulk at special discounts for sales
promotion, corporate gifts, fund-raising, or educational purposes. Special
editions can also be created to specifications. For details, contact the Special
Sales Department, Sky Pony Press, 307 West 36th Street, 11th Floor,
New York, NY 10018 or info@skyhorsepublishing.com.

Skyhorse® and Skyhorse Publishing® are registered trademark of Skyhorse Publishing, Inc.®, a Delaware corporation.

Visit our website at www.skyhorsepublishing.com.

10 9 8 7 6 5 4 3 2 1

Library of Congress Cataloging-in-Publication Data is available on file.

Cover design by Rattray Design

Print ISBN: 978-1-5107-2633-8

Printed in the United States of America

This book is dedicated to all the energetic, enthusiastic men, women, and children who help to make our world a better place by volunteering their time, talents, and money.

They are the richest people in the world.

Contents

Acknowledgments

Many people deserve a round of applause and my undying gratitude for the success of this book. To Jerry Pohlen for believing in my ability to write another book for Zephyr Press. To Lisa Rosenthal at Chicago Review Press for helping to clarify my project directions. To all the people that I interviewed in person, over the phone, and by e-mail—I thank you for your time and permission to use your story and picture. Your dedication to your charities overwhelms me. And to my husband, Doug, for his constant support and editorial comments during the planning and writing phases of this book.

Part I

General Information and Organization

Organizing kids to do anything can be daunting. Organizing them to do something they've never experienced can be *overwhelming*. This section provides many tips and ideas to help you plan, manage, and coordinate the children and the projects they undertake. See how leaders can motivate and stimulate their youthful members into action. Learn how to supervise with care and control. And find out how rewarding it is to help children become young philanthropists.

1

Put the "You" Back into Youth

Help Wanted

Young person to assist residents of local nursing home. Duties include reading to the blind, writing letters to relatives, and listening to stories of their childhoods. Must be available one day each month. Payment: none, except personal satisfaction.

D o you have young people at home, in school, or in your youth group who would instantly respond to this want ad with enthusiasm and a willingness to serve? If so, then your group is unique. Most children look for the paying jobs first so they can buy what they want with the money they earn. If they have money left over, they begin to look for a charity.

The mind-set for today's youth appears to be one of guided egoism. I say "guided" because most parents, leaders, and counselors help children to achieve whatever those children envision for themselves. That vision may be winning the soccer playoffs, reading a series of books, or performing in a recital. The children in your group probably do not fit into this category because you have already begun to help them see the value of philanthropy.

Where in their early education, either at home or school, do they learn to give back some of the gifts they have received? When do they understand that they should appreciate all that they have by helping those who don't have as much? Who teaches these lessons? You. As an adult working with young people, your job is formidable: get their minds off of themselves and onto the task of helping others.

When children think of others first, everyone benefits. There may be fewer fights in schools or more people to help in understaffed nursing homes. Children's boosted self-esteem might carry over to better class work and regular attendance. Philanthropy empowers children to be positive members of the community. According to Dorothy A. Johnson, president of the Council of Michigan Foundations, "The earlier we introduce the concept of giving and public service, the more successfully we incorporate these concepts into a child's daily behavior, and the greater the impact on society as a whole."

When we teach children the benefits of charitable projects, they are better prepared to meet the challenges of later life because they have helped others cope with similar challenges. Our nation has a foundation of philanthropy and volunteerism. According to the Points of Light Organization, 88 percent of persons sought by volunteer centers to assist with their programs are youth ages 6 to 18. However, these volunteers reflect only a small portion of all children in our country.

In addition, the number of girls versus boys who volunteer is unequal. According to the National Household Education survey, "Girls are more likely than boys to participate in volunteer activities. Fifty-seven percent of sixth- through twelfth-grade girls participated in 1999, compared with 47 percent of boys." As a result, we are further challenged to find suitable volunteer activities that will interest young boys.

Just as children need to learn how to change from a "me" to a "you" (or an "us") perspective, adults who work with children need to learn how to help facilitate this refocus. *Helping Kids Help* provides the framework and organization for youth leaders, teachers, parents, and counselors to foster philanthropy among the young, and to guide children in their philanthropic efforts. In this book, you will find ways to motivate young minds and stimulate young bodies into action.

The Many Benefits of Youth Philanthropy

"There is no limit to what can be accomplished if it doesn't matter who gets the credit." —Ralph Waldo Emerson

It is obvious that volunteerism and philanthropy help those in need. The advantages to the youth volunteers are not always so clear.

Life Skills

Whatever children learn when they are young generally carries through to their adult years. If they learn that you need to get all that you can to become successful, they will probably become greedy adults. If they learn that in helping others, they help themselves, these children are more likely to grow up to be responsible members of the greater community.

When children are responsible for the welfare of others, they learn the value of commitment. Teens learn punctuality when they see a senior citizen wait patiently for a visit and then be disappointed when the child is late.

Sacrificing time or money for a charitable cause shows the youth that his own personal desires may not be as critical as he once thought. It is gratifying to the youth and his parents when he spends a Saturday morning volunteering at a soup kitchen instead of playing video games. Everyone benefits.

Volunteering also teaches the child to budget her time wisely so that she can find time for her own activities and the charitable project. When young people are able to spend their time doing activities they value, they are less likely to cause problems for teachers, parents, and the community.

Teens who volunteer regularly become more self-assured in their own ability to make a difference in other people's lives. This enhanced personal power has personal benefits as well. Teens may seek out ways to help family members. They may be able to present oral reports with confidence. They will probably become proactive about their futures and contribute positively wherever they go.

When kids work in the community, they see people of many different ages and ethnicities. They learn that senior citizens have unique personalities like their friends, that people with a foreign heritage have amazing life stories to share, and that everyone is different and should be respected for those differences.

As someone who works with children, you know that a volunteerism ethic teaches children that one person can make a difference in the world. Whether helping to preserve the environment, assisting those in need, or saving abused animals, the young philanthropists learn life skills that positively impact their development. What a wonderful way to teach kids to be tolerant, caring, and organized!

About one tenth of the American work force is employed by volunteer organizations, not as volunteers, but as paid employees. Many of those employees began as volunteers.

Career Possibilities

When children volunteer, they are exposed to a variety of career options they may not have considered. They may find that their world of possibilities has expanded from what they see on television to what actually happens at a job. They can also learn a work ethic that many employers say is lacking in today's employees. In 2002, Dr. Andrew Brod, in cooperation with the United Way of Greater Greensboro, North Carolina, surveyed employers to find out what they most wanted to see in new hires. Using 11 categories, they found that what employers wanted and what prospective employees presented were not always the same.

Category	Rank by Importance to Employer	Rank as Presented by Entry-Level Employees
Integrity and honesty (IH)	1	4
Oral communication (OC)	2	1
Learning and reasoning skills (LRS)	3	5
Self-management (SM)	4	8
Written communication (WC)	5	6
Social skills (SS)	6	3
Problem-solving and decision-making (PSD)	7	10
Information-Technology skills (IT)	8	2
Creative thinking (CT)	9	7
Math/Arithmetic skills (MA)	10	9
Management/Leadership (ML)	11	11

From the results of Dr. Brod's survey, we can conclude that the youth of today have learned how to speak well and use technology. However, their management, problem-solving skills, and math abilities are somewhat lacking. The good news is that their social skills and integrity are still high on the list. In other words, they can effectively work with others but are reluctant to be self-starters when presented with a unique problem.

Consider this scenario about a young man who volunteers at the local animal shelter on Saturday mornings. The skills he learns from Dr. Brod's research are indicated in parentheses.

Jacob awakens to his alarm set for 6:15 (SM). He knows the animals will be hungry when he arrives at the shelter at 7:00. He checks in with the supervisor and prints his list of animals and their daily food requirements from the computer (IT). He asks what happened to "Jingles" because he isn't on the list (LRS). The supervisor explains that Jingles was adopted. Jacob asks about the people who adopted him (OC), then goes to the kennels. There he finds a Lab puppy scratching her ear. He tells the supervisor that the puppy might have an ear infection (PSD). The supervisor thanks Jacob for his observation. After feeding and watering the rest of the animals, he records (WC) the time of feeding and the amount given, adding the columns so the supervisor can see the running total of food given over the week (MA).

The supervisor brings in a new volunteer, Sasha, for Jacob to familiarize with the routine. He finds out that she moved to their neighborhood from Russia four years ago. He is careful to speak slowly so she can understand him (SS). While showing her around, he accidentally bumps into a shelf and knocks down a bottle of flea dip. It shatters on the floor. Excusing himself from Sasha, he cleans up the mess, then reports the incident to the supervisor (IH). Back with Sasha, Jacob allows her to name the new puppy so she will feel connected to the animal shelter (ML). Finally, he sees that Sasha wants to begin her service project, so he asks her to teach him a Russian song while they work to pass the time more quickly (CT).

So, Jacob may be simply trying to get a date with the new girl who came to work with him. He's nervous and clumsy as any teenager might be. Yet, in that one morning of volunteer work, he learned and demonstrated the 11 characteristics that employers seek in their employees.

In addition to learning career ethics, young volunteers learn that organizations, even volunteer organizations, have a hierarchy of employment. They see that there are management positions that require advanced degrees and there are other positions that are available for entry-level workers. In between is a broad spectrum of employees who have varying degrees of responsibility, education, and income.

There are opportunities for young people to learn leadership skills by serving on student advisory boards. They can exercise their oral communication skills by joining lobby groups for specific causes. Even the youngest of volunteers learns job-related skills when she collects "Toys for Tots" during the holidays.

Young people learn that in most cases a higher education results in higher pay, more respect, and more responsibility. They learn that there are opportunities for employment that are outside of their realms of experience, that they can intern for a philanthropic organization and gain college credits, and that volunteer and paid employment opportunities abound for individuals with integrity and organizational skills in the service organizations.

2

A Leader's Guide to Children at Meetings

"Only a life lived for others is a life worthwhile."

—Albert Einstein

Whether you lead a religious-based or a general-interest group of children, the problems that they bring to your group are universal. Don't expect your children or teens to arrive with a clean slate, ready to do charitable projects. Instead, expect some to come with medical problems, or to be stressed, angry, aggressive, or depressed. Then, if your group arrives with none of these, you will be pleasantly surprised.

Medical Problems

Some children are on medication to treat an ongoing condition; others are temporarily taking antibiotics for an infection. In either case, you are legally bound to not administer the medication unless you are a registered nurse and obtain prior permission from the parents to give the medication to the child. However, in the absence of a registered nurse, the child may self-administer the medication, provided the parent grants written permission to do so, and the medication is in its original container. The law is very specific about non-medical personnel administering medications, even non-prescription medications, to children. Be very careful how you handle this situation. You may want to ask the parent to return to your group meeting when a young child needs her medication to avoid legal problems.

What do you do with ADHD children? Keep them busy. They prefer to be mentally and physically active. If your group is formally organized, encourage them to run for an office so they will be busy throughout the meeting. Unless you help your ADHD kids to focus by calling their names frequently, you will lose their attention quickly. If you need an errand run, pair the ADHD child with one who usually stays focused. If you need a child to organize and label boxes, the ADHD child may take longer to do this task because he is constantly distracted, but the job will get done eventually and he will be kept busy. ADHD children are generally extremely creative and can be counted on to develop new and interesting ideas during brainstorming sessions. Use their gifts so they fulfill their potential and you will have few problems with their inability to stay focused.

When you plan snacks, remember to ask ahead of time about food allergies. Some children are extremely allergic to peanuts and other legumes. I had one child whose mother told me she was allergic to peanuts, so we planned snacks without nuts. Then we did an environmental project that involved peanut butter on pinecones. I consulted her mother in advance, and she did not think it would cause an allergic reaction. We did the project, careful to wash her hands afterward. Five minutes later, we noticed a rash traveling up her arm from the top of where we had washed her hands. I called her mother, who rushed over with the Epi-pen to stop the allergic reaction before it reached her throat. To this day, I am very, very careful about all food allergies.

Then there are the kids who are allergic to bee stings, but don't know it because they've never been stung. Imagine being on an outdoor project when one person in your group gets stung. The arm begins to swell at an alarming rate. You're miles from the nearest hospital. Your first aid kit is not equipped to handle an allergic reaction such as this. What do you do? What should you have done? First, you should have instructed all of your members to avoid bright clothing and scented toiletries. They should have applied insect repellent, too. You should have packed emergency bee sting vials, available over the counter, and an ice pack that becomes cold when activated, which is good for a number of ailments in addition to bee stings. If a child is having an allergic reaction, call 911 immediately.

Some of your children may be asthmatic. They usually know their limitations and will carry a rescue inhaler with them. When they feel an attack coming on, they can take the recommended number of puffs from their inhaler to stop a major attack. However, make sure you have obtained permission from the parents to allow the child to self-medicate. Most states allow self-medication for asthma because it can mean the difference between life and death. If you know that one of the children in your group is asthmatic, keep that child away from known triggers—dust, dirt, mold, and extreme exercise. If you see him using a rescue inhaler, call the parents or 911 immediately, as a major attack may not be far in the future.

ADHD, bee sting allergy, and asthma are the most common medical issues that you will encounter when working with a group of children. However, there are many other problems that children bring with them. It's a good idea to have their parents complete a medical history form. Take a first aid course so you know what to do in an emergency. Be prepared for anything, and you'll be able to assure the safety of the children in your charge.

Emotional Problems

Due to incidents that happen at home, in school, and with friends, children and teens sometimes bring emotional problems with them to group meetings. They may be angry, aggressive, stressed, or depressed. Each of these issues should be handled only superficially at the group meeting to minimize disruption to the project. Do not attempt to provide therapy sessions for the troubled youth; leave that to the professionals.

What can you do to help these emotionally troubled children at meetings? First, acknowledge them with a simple statement such as, "Jim, I can see that you're angry about something. Try to put that in the back of your mind while we do our project planning today." Don't ignore that the child is angry, but don't make a big deal out of it, either. By acknowledging his emotional instability in a simple manner, you have satisfied his desire for attention without buying into the problem.

Your program of charitable projects is a good outlet for these aggressive or depressed children. It helps take their minds off their own problems by guiding them to focus on other people's problems. They can see that they're not alone in this world, and they may also become aware of how others are coping with issues that are probably more severe than their own. Certainly, the child who is dealing with the divorce of his parents is coping by becoming depressed or aggressive. But when she sees that others have no food or shelter, it may help to put her problems into perspective.

During group meetings, play peaceful music in the background, rather than the loud music that they may prefer. Be firm about this. They may ask you to change the CD at first, but eventually they will come to expect the calming background music. If you always meet at the same location, you could add a water feature such as a fish tank or a cascading fountain. Do whatever you can to make your meeting space one that welcomes the stressed, aggressive, depressed, or angry youth into your environment.

Teach by example. If you become frustrated with the slow progress that your group is making, don't show it. Remain calm and the kids will remain calm. If you find yourself becoming angry, leave the room for a moment. Take a bathroom break. Splash water on your face, count to 10, or tell yourself that the situation is only temporary. As soon as the kids leave, you can go back to your normal routine. Laugh frequently. Tell jokes. Tell stories. Laughter is a great stress reducer and icebreaker if there is a tense moment. Just take care not to laugh at a child or the situation will become worse.

"The value of compassion cannot be over-emphasized. Anyone can criticize. It takes a true believer to be compassionate. No greater burden can be borne by an individual than to know no one cares or understands." —Arthur H. Stainback

Group-Building Activities

Before you attempt to do any projects, the group needs to consider itself a unit. Sometimes you will have members from diverse backgrounds who don't know each other. Other times, you will have members who know each other slightly, but who are reluctant to take the first step. Here are a few suggestions for getting young people to know each other better before developing a project plan. They all require little or no effort and planning by the leader. Name tags, either purchased or made, will help group members get to know each other by name more quickly.

Guidelines for Group-Building Activities

- For children in middle and high school, don't call the activities games or mixers, or any similar-sounding name. These can be a turn-off for older kids. Just begin by saying what to do first, such as, "When everyone is seated in a circle, we can begin."

- Always be prepared for the activities. Children sense when you are unsure of yourself.
- Play the game with the kids—remember, the leader is part of the group, too.
- Make the explanation short and to the point.
- Laugh and enjoy the game with the kids.

Toilet Paper Pull-Off

This is my all-time favorite icebreaker and group builder. It is unique and generally not repeated in other organizations, so the kids don't know what to expect. Use one single roll of toilet paper for each 10 members. Pass the rolls around. Tell students to pull off the number of sheets that equals _____ (fill in the blank). You could say: "the number of senior citizen homes in the area," or "the number of vacant lots that need cleaning," or "the number of animal shelters in the area," and so on. When they are done giggling about passing around toilet paper and judging how many sheets the other kids have torn off, tell them, "Now, for each sheet, share one thing about yourself with the group." After the groans have subsided, help them to consider what to say: the number of people in their family, their middle name, their favorite performer or sport, where they were born, and so forth.

Yarn Ball Toss

Begin with a ball of yarn—yes, a ball, not a skein as purchased at a craft store. Arrange the group in a circle, facing toward the center. Give one person the ball of yarn. He holds onto the loose end, tells one thing about himself, and then tosses the ball to someone else. She holds onto a piece of yarn, tells something about herself, and then tosses the ball of yarn to another person in the circle. Each player, in turn, holds onto a part of the yarn to create a web joining the group together. Tell the kids to remember what everyone shares about themselves. The only rule is that a player must toss it to another player who has not yet shared with the group. After everyone has had one turn, do another round. This time it is more difficult. Instead of saying something about themselves, the members have to say what another person said before tossing the yarn ball to that person. If a player can't remember, he tosses the ball to anyone, who then offers hints until he can remember what she said about herself. After the second round is complete, point out how joined the group has become because they have formed a web in the middle of the circle.

Find Someone Else Who . . .

This is your typical first day of camp or school mixer game with a twist. Reproduce the sheet on page 19, have the kids answer each question, find someone else with the same answer to initial the last column, then return to the circle of seats when they have the paper complete or whenever you signal time is up. Discuss similarities among the group. When you collect these sheets, it becomes a helpful tool for dividing the members into subgroups with similar interests and abilities.

Although it may take some time to set up, you could use these surveys to develop a computer database for your group members' names and interests. Then, when you need to group by ability, you can do a simple computer sort rather than a sheet-by-sheet hand sort.

Four Corners Variation

If you have a group that would rather be active than sit and play games, then try this Four Corners game. It uses up youthful energy and gets the kids to know each other at the same time, but involves a little preparation on your part.

Get four pieces of poster board. Hold them vertically. At the top, label each 1, 2, 3, or 4 in large numbers. Write one number on the top half of each piece of poster board. Then, on regular-sized sheets of paper, write one of the options to each of the statements before the colon below or create your own statements with four options.

- My favorite color is: red, green, purple, blue
- I prefer to: read, fish, play video games, talk to my friends
- My favorite books are: biographies, mysteries, nonfiction, romances (or change to "animal stories" if playing with younger groups)
- My favorite food is: macaroni and cheese, chocolate chip cookies, hot dogs, ice cream
- My favorite class in school is: science, math, reading, history
- My favorite sport is: basketball, hockey, football, baseball
- I would like to volunteer with: children, senior citizens, animals, any other group

Make four stacks of these options, each containing one answer to each statement. Be sure to place these in the same order for each set. Mount one stack of answers to the bottom half of each piece of poster board. Place one poster board in each corner of the room. After each round, pull off the top sheet, leaving the next group of categories.

To play the game, choose someone to cover her eyes and count to 15. While she is counting, the rest of the group scrambles to the corner containing the option that most closely indicates each person's opinion. When the counter is done, she calls out a number between one and four. The players who are in that corner, who chose that number, sit down. After each round, the leader tears off the top category, revealing the next category and four different responses for the next round. The play continues with other categories and responses until there are four or fewer players left. Then, they

Your Name _____		Answer-Buddy's
Question	**Your Answer**	**Initials**
Have you ever volunteered before?		
How many years have you been volunteering?		
Do you like reading to children?		
Do you enjoy working outside?		
Do you prefer working with your hands, your brain, or both?		
What is your favorite thing to do when you're not in school?		
Who was your favorite teacher?		
What is your favorite class in school?		
Have you ever sold anything for a fundraiser? What?		
Are you good with computer programs?		
Do you like to write letters?		
Are you organized?		
Do you like to draw?		
Do you like to perform in plays?		
Can you sew or quilt?		
Do you do scrapbooking?		
What is your favorite sport to play?		
Do you like to garden?		
How many pets do you have?		
Do you like math class?		

pay no attention to the category signs, only the numbers. The counter counts and each player must be at a different corner by the time the counter is done. The person at the number announced by the counter sits down. Again, this continues until there is only one person left—the winner, who would become the counter for the next round.

Naturally, any of these games could be played outside, sitting on the grass or on mats. If you play the Four Corners Variation game outside, bring chairs for attaching the posters. Also, I recommend not playing the toilet paper game outside on a windy day!

Remember, competition games that involve teams are divisive. If you look in books or on the Internet for other games to play, make sure the group has a single goal.

Writing the Mission Statement

The last way to build your members into a solid group, after all the games have been played, is to build a Mission Statement. This is essential for staying on track if the group loses focus. It should provide the members a vision into the future so they can visualize a successful group project before any activities begin. At the end of your first group-building meeting, send the members home with ideas for ways to develop a Mission Statement. Then use the steps below as a guide to develop the group's Mission Statement.

Step One Create a name for your group. It could be an acronym, such as KIDS (Kids in Detroit Serve), or a simple description of your group—St. David's Youth Group. I find that a creative name is more effective than the simple description. It also makes for a fun T-shirt design project.

Step Two Develop a list of words that identify why you meet as a group. These words might include help, clean, assist, care, and so forth.

Step Three Write a one-sentence description of the group.

Step Four Make a list of community or international needs that your group has identified.

Step Five Write the one-paragraph Mission Statement, using group consensus. Be positive, general, concise, and simple, so the statement may be loosely interpreted for any occasion.

Here are two examples of Mission Statements:

> The Indiana 4-H's mission is to assist youth and adults in their development by conducting hands-on educational programs, using the knowledge base of Purdue University, other land grant universities, and the United States Department of Agriculture.

Boys and Girls Clubs is a youth-serving organization dedicated to enhancing and assisting young people in realizing and developing the essential skills for living through the promotion of health, social, educational, vocational, leadership, and character development experiences.

If you are having difficulty developing a working mission statement, you can start by filling in the blanks here.

The mission of _____ is to promote _____
for _____. Through _____
and _____, we will actively participate in projects that follow
the model established by _____.

When you have built a cohesive group, and written and posted your mission statement, you are finally ready to begin working on a project. Just as priming and sanding are essential for painting, the group-building activities and mission statement writing are essential to a successful youth philanthropy effort.

3

Getting Started

"Compassion is not religious business, it is human business, it is not luxury, it is essential for our own peace and mental stability, it is essential for human survival."

—Dalai Lama

This chapter helps you to formally incorporate your group if you feel that is necessary. You will find suggestions for guiding your children to decide which philanthropic project is best for them. Finally, you will learn how to handle the fundamentals of coordinating and evaluating a youth philanthropic project.

Should You File for 501(c)(3) Status?

If you have a group of kids who meet informally in your dining room to engage in philanthropic efforts, then skip to the next section in this chapter. However, if you are looking to create a formal, organized, nonprofit organization of juvenile members with adult leaders, then this first section is for you.

You could incorporate your nonprofit 501(c)(3) organization by filing articles of incorporation with your state attorney general's office or the division of taxation. Here are the reasons to incorporate your nonprofit organization:

- To enable the organization to own property and have its own bank account.
- To ensure that the organization can stand on its own, even after the founding members are gone.
- To protect yourself from liability.
- To allow the formation of a board of directors to oversee the operation of the organization.

To find out about the guidelines in your state go to the Internet and, using your favorite search engine, type in " _____ state attorney" with the name of your state in place of the blank. One of the first few Web sites to appear will be the office for your state. The site will detail whether you need to file with the division of taxation or the attorney general's office. You may also find a document that outlines the steps you need to take and the fees involved.

If you want tax-exempt status, you should file with the IRS. The IRS states that you must be a corporation, community chest, fund, or foundation to receive tax-exempt status. Although you can fill out the paperwork yourself, it's a good idea to have legal counsel to guard against being considered by the government as a for-profit organization that is bound to pay taxes. The IRS publication #557, *Tax Exempt Status for Your Organization*, is very helpful.

Being a nonprofit organization with tax-exempt status is a complex process that is better left to larger organizations. I'm assuming that if you're reading this book, you're simply looking for ways to organize the children in your care who are looking for ways to help the community, so read on to see how to proceed.

But if you want a more in-depth discussion about nonprofit incorporation, check out *Starting and Building a Nonprofit: A Practical Guide* by Peri Pakroo (Berkeley, CA: NOLO Publishing, 2005) or *How to Form a Nonprofit Corporation* by Anthony Mancuso, 7th edition (Berkeley, CA: NOLO Publishing, 2005). For a lighter, more humorous, but still practical approach, read *Everything You Never Wanted to Know About Your Nonprofit Corporation* by Ms. Cellaneous, the Unknown Attorney (Bellissima Publishing, 2005).

How to Choose Your Philanthropy

When children have a role in the selection of their philanthropic project, they will be more inclined to participate in it. However, if you simply ask, "What do you want to do?" you may get 20 blank stares or receive 20 different answers. In this section, you will find ideas for creatively brainstorming projects until you narrow the selections down to one or two workable ideas.

Step One: Involve the Children in the Selection Process

Many times children have little choice in their lives. They are told to eat their vegetables, to stay in the backyard, or to do their homework. However, when they are given options to consider and have input to that list of options, they will be more likely to take ownership of their projects. Children love to make their own choices, whether it is which breakfast cereal to eat, when to do their homework, or which philanthropic project to choose.

Children also like to play games. Here are a few games you can play that will get your children thinking about service projects and help them select one.

Air Mail

Ask the children to write an idea for a philanthropic project on a piece of paper. Then, have them fold the paper into the shape of an airplane. You may offer suggestions for airplane designs or you may let them design their own. After everyone has their planes folded, have them sail their planes around the room to others in the classroom. When another child picks up the plane, he unfolds it and writes a comment under the original idea. Only positive comments are allowed, which could include how to raise money, what to do, and why it is a good project. After you repeat this process five times, sit in a circle and read the children's ideas and comments. After all are read, discuss which one will be your project for the month, semester, or year.

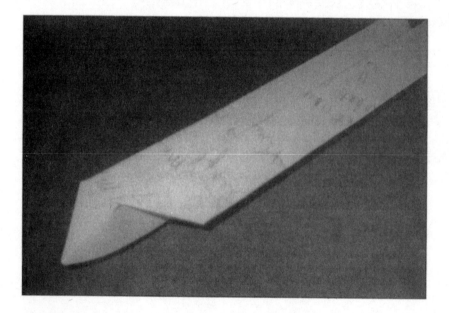

Game Show

Use the chart on page 27 to jump-start a discussion of various philanthropic projects. (Or you may create your own chart for projects in your area.) Using a die or spinner, roll or spin to select a number from each column. Discuss how the combined ideas could be implemented. Some of the ideas will be funny and unworkable; others will be definitely workable. Try several combinations before you settle on one that the group finds agreeable. Any way you look at it, the kids will have fun discussing their potential projects.

#	Target	#	How to Earn Money	#	What to Do
1	Senior citizens	1	Raffle	1	Write
2	Animals	2	Bake Sale	2	Record
3	Environment	3	Garage Sale	3	Collect
4	Children	4	Craft Sale	4	Create
5	Military	5	Car Wash	5	Adopt a
6	Handicapped	6	_____-a-thon	6	Help

For example, if you pick this combination—environment, bake sale, and write (letters)—it could lead to a discussion of a themed bake sale and a letter-writing campaign to help clean up a vacant lot. Or perhaps you choose this combination—senior citizens, car wash, and record (stories). This might lead your children to discuss the special needs of senior citizens. They would videotape their carwash and show it to the senior citizens, and then donate tapes of the children reading their favorite books. The money raised would pay for the tapes and player. Who could resist youthful voices reading *The Cat in the Hat*?

Story Time

From magazines or the Internet, collect pictures of people, places, or animals that might have already benefited from a philanthropic effort. In groups of two or three, the children will develop a story about what was needed and how it was accomplished. If the project was for a person, how did the person feel after the project was completed? When you use pictures to jump-start the discussion, children find it easier to come up with a story and related projects.

Step Two: Decide Whether You Want to Help at Home or Globally

Certainly, children will see the fruits of their efforts if you decide to visit the local nursing home or read to children in hospitals. However, sometimes children want to do something for the greater good that benefits people outside of their immediate community. They may want to do something about world hunger or write letters to military personnel. Encourage your group to list their reasons for selecting a charitable project then discuss those reasons with the group. For example, you may have a member whose father serves in the military and she knows that the men who serve with him need magazines, chewing gum, and playing cards. If you have no special cases such as this example in your group, then here's one way to help them decide. Place a picture of the genie from *Aladdin* or a picture of a magic lamp on a bulletin board. What three wishes that would help solve a local or world problem would the children ask of the genie? Post and discuss their answers.

Step Three: Evaluate the Charity's Effectiveness and Worth

If you are considering donating time or money to a nonprofit organization, it is important to evaluate the effectiveness of the foundation. There are three types of foundations: public, private, and independent.

Public foundations are those that support individual communities. Local *freeholders,* who are county administrators, or other political persons, generally run public foundations. Other public foundations are those run by service clubs such as the Rotary, Moose, and Elks.

There are three types of *private foundations*: Family, Corporate, and Independent. Family foundations, such as the Bill and Melinda Gates Foundation, are operated by family members for specific charitable projects. Bill Gates, founder of Microsoft, with his wife, Melinda, provides funds for scholarships and research on children's diseases. It is the largest charitable foundation, donating more than one billion dollars each year. Major companies, such as the Ford Motor Company, operate corporate foundations as a side venture. In 1936, Henry Ford established the Ford Foundation to support the Henry Ford Hospital and the Henry Ford Museum, a collection of Ford's memorabilia. After his death, the family decided to use the foundation to promote peace, freedom, and education throughout the world. The focus of the foundation has little to do with the corporation— selling cars. It is a side venture which allows the Ford family to use some of its profits for the greater good.

Independent foundations usually began as family or corporate foundations, but the original family no longer serves on the board or the founding corporation no longer exists. An example of an independent foundation is the Kresge Foundation. In 1924, Sebastian Kresge established the Kresge Foundation for the simple purpose of promoting the well-being of mankind. By the time he died in 1966, he had given the foundation over $60 million. No longer controlled by members of the Kresge family, it is now worth over $2.7 billion and supports the work of smaller foundations.

In order to determine the effectiveness of a foundation and whether it is worthy of your efforts, find out the answers to the following questions:

- *What percentage of the income actually reaches those in need of assistance?* They should have at least 65 percent of their funds going directly to the program and less than 35 percent for administrative costs and fundraising activities.
- *Does the foundation publish an annual financial report that has been reviewed by an auditor?* If the foundation's gross income is over $250,000, a formal audit is required. Under $250,000 gross income, a

CPA should review their finances. Under $100,000, an internal audit is acceptable. Whatever the income of your organization, it is important to audit the finances so the membership knows that the money is being used for its intended purpose.

- *What projects does the foundation pursue, and how would your children support that effort?* Some foundations only accept money, while others will accept individual efforts to help support their causes.
- *Do the administrators have a phone number, e-mail, or snail mail address listed on their Web site or in their informational brochure?* Beware if there is no way to easily contact the administrators, because that may mean that they are disreputable.
- *What percentage of the board members are paid for their participation?* No more than 10 percent of the total number of board members should be in this category. Also, look to see if the paid members are treasurers or the chairperson. If that is the case, it is easier, but hopefully not more likely, for them to skim funds for their own purposes.
- *Have there been any complaints against the organization?* Go to www.give.org to see a list of organizations and the information that has been provided to the Better Business Bureau (BBB). Or you can see if your potential charity has the BBB Wise Giving Alliance Standards seal, which indicates that the charity has met the BBB accountability standards and is reliable.
- *What is the foundation's mission statement?* Is it consistent with your children's goals for charitable giving?

In addition to foundations, there are countless other organizations that will accept both money and time. When you are evaluating the effectiveness of an organization, always ask yourself why it is worthy of your efforts. Use this chart to evaluate organizations at home and those that affect the larger community. One example has been provided for you.

Name of Organization	Who or What Does It Benefit?	What Does the Organization Need?	How Would You Provide the Charity?	What Drawbacks Are There?
Booksforsoldiers.com	Military at home and overseas	Books, magazines, and supplies	Collection of books and magazines	Shipping costs for mailing the magazines

"To give without any reward, or any notice, has a special quality of its own."

—*Anne Morrow Lindbergh*

Problems You Might Encounter

As with any group, whether it is children or adults, problems will occur. When leaders anticipate and prevent problems, the group will function more smoothly. Hopefully, you won't encounter any of the problems presented in this section, but if you do, you'll be prepared.

Some Children Don't Want to Be Charitable

When you begin a campaign to have kids understand the benefits of charitable giving and then involve them in a project, remember that not everyone wants to be charitable. Some children only want to raise money for themselves. They want a new video game or a bicycle and might not understand that there are those who don't even have enough food to eat. See the Resources Section on page 153 for books and videos that may create interest among such students. You can also try this exercise:

Begin by playing Louis Armstrong's "Wonderful World." While it is playing, have the kids list all the things that they want for themselves—toys, games, clothes, and more. They may discuss their wants with their friends to create their list. Then, when the song is over, have them list on a separate sheet of paper all the things they already have that less fortunate children might enjoy but do not have. This time, they need to be absolutely quiet and create their list without anyone's help.

Once students complete their lists then discuss the following:

- How are the two lists different?
- How important are your wants compared with the needs of children who have less?
- Which makes you feel better: to give or to receive?
- Would you be willing to give up some of your wants to help fulfill someone else's needs?

When you are done with this discussion, you can usually go on to discuss how you might best use your philanthropic energy. Ask the children to express their feelings. Are they now tuned in to the needs of others? Are they exercising their empathy muscles? In this way, even children who have very little will be able to find philanthropic projects to help children (or adults, or animals, and so forth) who have even less than they do.

Help the children visualize what it would look like to do a charitable project. Provide them with paper and new crayons for their new way of thinking about doing projects for others. Have them draw what they envision. Hang their pictures in your classroom, meeting space, or home. If you have children who are unable or unwilling to draw, they can cut and paste pictures from magazines or print out and cut out pictures from the Internet. When you are done with your philanthropic project, have them draw another picture and compare the before and after images and attitudes.

Some People Do Not Trust Altruism in Children

Just as some children do not understand the importance of charitable giving, some adults may not trust that children are raising money for someone else. Picture four preteen kids in front of a grocery store with a can labeled "United Way." Would you trust that the kids are actually giving all of the money they collect to the yearly campaign? Probably not. Now picture four Girl Scouts with cookies and a leader standing in front of that same grocery store. Would you trust that the cookie money would reach the Girl Scout headquarters? You probably would. What is the difference between the two fundraising efforts? Both were nationally accepted charities. However, in the second scenario, an adult was present and merchandise was involved. If you want adults to have confidence that the kids are trustworthy, you need those two components: adult presence and merchandise or services for the donation.

Plan for the Safety and Security of Children

You certainly know that children should not go alone selling products door-to-door for fundraisers. So, what can you do to ensure the safety of the children in your group? Here are some ideas:

- Have parents assist children with making a list of trusted friends, neighbors, and relatives. Include in that list phone numbers, addresses, and e-mail addresses. When you have a fundraiser, only contact these people.
- Never allow children to collect money unless accompanied by an adult.
- Have a catalog fundraiser, and allow parents to take the catalog to work or meetings.
- Never carry large amounts of cash. As the adults collect money, have them deposit it in a bank account designated for your group. Encourage patrons to write checks made out to the group or beneficiary of the fundraiser.
- Don't sell products or solicit money at stop signs and transportation stations.
- Tell children not to enter anyone's house.
- Have parents sign an agreement to accompany their children during all fundraising activities.
- Make sure the children understand that safety is more important than the amount of money they raise.
- Make sure younger children have memorized their home address and phone number. It also helps if they know the phone number of a trusted family member, such as a grandparent.
- For maximum security, a child can carry a cell phone that may be used in an emergency.

In addition to the suggestions above, children need to learn how to protect themselves if they happen to find themselves in a difficult situation despite all the precautions. It's like a school fire drill, except it prepares them for real-life emergencies. Provide the children in your care with a role-play situation using these scenarios (the suggested responses are in parentheses):

- A stranger approaches the child on the street. The parent is not as close as he or she should be. (It's OK to scream and say, "No" as loudly as possible.)
- Someone tries to grab the child and pull her into a car. (Stay further away than grabbing distance.)
- A neighbor invites the child into their home. (Politely refuse. Never trust anyone, even neighbors, unless the parent accompanies the child.)
- The child feels as if he is being followed. (Never run. Go to an area where there are many people and ask for help.)
- A policeman offers to help the child get home. (Imposters can easily obtain uniforms. Never accept help until an adult known to the child verifies the authenticity of the policeman.)

Background and Drug Checks

If you hire employees, you may want to consider getting background checks. This is also important to guard against lawsuits. More than a dozen Boys and Girls Clubs have begun using the services available at www.verified person.com. This New York-based company constantly updates its database of convicted felons and pedophiles. Other online sources are available as well. Here's a good idea: encourage your employees to obtain their own background checks and add that to their applications. At www.choicetrust.com, for example, potential employees can get a background check for under $30. Drug testing supplies are available over the counter at most pharmacies.

If you don't ask potential employees to provide their own background checks, make sure you obtain written permission from them before doing a background or drug check. As with any employer, you could also ask for a list of character references and previous employment contacts. Remember that the background and drug checks are for your peace of mind when hiring paid employees using foundation money. Generally, volunteers do not need to undergo such scrutiny.

Supervision—How Much Is Too Much?

The children will rebel and lose interest in the project if they feel they are being told what to do too frequently. Although it is tempting to step in and do some of the work or organization for the kids, ultimately it is their project.

One way to give back some control to the group is to have them create a responsibility chart. They decide who will bring snacks and at whose house the next meeting will be held. They decide who will call the contact persons for your project and who will ask parents for transportation. Your job as leader is to sit back, watch, and listen. There are only a few times when you should step in. One is when their safety could be compromised; another is when the group is getting off track and needs to be reminded of their purpose.

That's not to say that you can't offer guided choices to help with their decision-making process. For example, perhaps the children are having difficulty deciding which kind of philanthropic project to pursue. You could offer them a series of choices: Senior citizens or children? Animals or the environment? Homelessness or the military? Once they have picked one of the two choices in each group, go back and combine the choices (children or animals) until only one is left. This works for a lot of other decisions, as well, and the children have the sense that they have determined their philanthropic path by themselves.

Sometimes you can enlist the aid of older children to help younger children. If there is a teen youth group looking for a charitable project, your younger group of eight-year-olds could become their charitable project. In the end, young people learn from teens, cooperating on their philanthropic project. It's a win-win situation.

How to Find the Time and Space for Philanthropy

"Some people give time, some money, some their skills and con- nections, some literally give their life's blood. But everyone has something to give." —Barbara Bush

Finding Time

You and the children in your group are busy. You might transport kids to soccer games, piano lessons, and ballet class. They are engaged in those activ- ities. You go to work; they go to school. You clean the house and mow the lawn; they do homework and school projects. How do you find the time for philanthropic projects?

The first step is to take a good look at your schedules. Most people have empty time spent in less altruistic endeavors, such as talking on the phone or watching television. Look at the sample schedule on page 38.

At first glance, this appears to be a full weekday schedule with no time left over for philanthropic pursuits. Look again. When the kids come home, they can do their homework instead of sending messages to friends. That will free up the 7:00 to 8:00 time slot for charitable projects. Instead of watching television at 8:00, adults could clean up the kitchen at that time while they work on the charitable projects with the kids from 7:00 to 8:00. This also has the benefit of a shared family project and time spent working together. Yes, it requires commitment and a desire to help for a schedule like that to work.

Time	Adult Schedule	Child Schedule
6:00	Get up, get ready, have breakfast	Get up, get ready, have breakfast
7:00	Go to work	Wait for the bus, go to school
8:00–3:00	Work (some adults will have a different schedule)	School
3:00	Still at work	Snack, check e-mail, IM friends
4:00	Still at work	Soccer practice; piano lessons
5:00	Pick up kids from practice, make dinner	More practice, then shower
6:00	Eat dinner	Eat dinner
7:00	Clean up kitchen, put in a load of wash, and so forth	Do homework
8:00	Watch television, read, relax	Watch television or do more homework
9:00	Get ready for bed, sleep	Get ready for bed, sleep

The weekends are usually less hectic, so you could spend the extra weekday time planning for actual project work on the weekends. However, if you and your children spend even a little time every day on your philanthropic project, you will all accomplish much more. Help the kids to understand that they will feel good about themselves and their accomplishments every day, not just on the weekends.

When people work together, they can accomplish much more than one person working alone. Unless you already lead or teach a group of children, consider forming a weekend club of three to six children to work together on a philanthropic project.

At your first club meeting, decide:

- Will the meetings always be held at the same home or will they rotate through the homes of the club members? Suggestion: Sometimes it is

easiest, depending on you project, to stay at one house where the supplies may be stored.

- Who will provide the snacks? Suggestion: Rotate the snack duty through the club members. Encourage healthy snacks by offering ice cream occasionally if they eat fruit or similarly nutritious snacks at the other meetings.

- Will you have a president, treasurer, and secretary? Suggestion: Having a president indicates that one person carries all the power and the rest do not. However, a secretary is important for recording progress and a treasurer can keep track of the finances.

- How often will the club meet? Suggestion: At first, there will be plenty of enthusiasm, so the children may want to meet every weekend for a month to kick off the project. After that, they should meet once or twice a month unless the enthusiasm warrants weekly meetings.

- Will you charge dues? Suggestion: If your project needs money up front, then you might charge dues to belong. However, consider whether at least one person is financially unable to contribute. If that is the case, no one should be obligated to pay dues. Instead, have your first activity be a simple fundraiser.

Involving other parents in the project will help provide additional support to sustain the group, too.

Finding Space

In today's homes, there is usually an accumulated clutter from 10 or more years of living together as a family. In the classrooms, there is an accumulated clutter from over 20 years of teaching. Ours is a cluttered society. The first step to finding storage for your charitable projects is to clear out the clutter.

Here's a great idea: clear the clutter, have a yard sale to earn money for your project, and replace the cluttered area with storage boxes for your supplies. However, you will need a plan and timeline for clearing the clutter. What accumulated over a number of years will not disappear in only a few days. Begin with three trash bags. Label them:

- Trash (This will probably be your largest collection!)
- Relocate (Make sure you save time to actually put the things where they belong.)
- Give away or sell at a yard sale. (If you're not having one at your home, find a place where you can buy space.)

Make your decluttering fun. Enlist the aid of your children—they will learn valuable organizational skills. Put on music. Dance to the beat as you remove stuff from the corner you have designated for philanthropy storage.

When you are done, dust the shelves if you have them and vacuum the area. Now you are ready to reorganize for your philanthropy.

Since you want to use most of your money for the project, not for storage supplies, here are some free or inexpensive ideas for storage:

- Use heavy cardboard boxes instead of purchased storage bins. (Go to liquor stores—their boxes are usually fairly sturdy.)
- Within those cardboard boxes, and for further organization, add empty cereal boxes that the kids have decorated by gluing paper to the front and labeling what's in them. Also label the tops so you can see in an instant what's inside. When arranged sideways instead of vertically, they may be used as drawers.
- Search yard sales for useful items such as in-box trays that may be used to organize construction paper.
- Empty baby wipes containers are wonderful for storing small items such as beads, and they stack! Label the front and sides for easy identification.
- For medium sized items, shoeboxes work well.
- Sometimes it's just practical to purchase one of those metal workshop storage shelves. They are relatively inexpensive and do the job nicely.
- Store small items in zippered plastic bags. But don't stack them in a box. Instead, using duct tape, tape the bottom of the bag to the bottom of a wire hanger. Place your items in the bag, zip it up, then hang it. (See the next bullet point for an idea on where to hang them.)
- To organize hanging items, find a tri-fold room-divider screen at a yard sale. Paint the wood, if you wish, then cover each section with chicken wire. Voila—instant hanging space for those zippered bags on hangers. If you have one side cloth covered, it can also serve as a room divider or shield for your storage area.

4

The Money Bit: Fund Raising and Managing

"If every American donated five hours a week, it would equal the labor of 20 million full-time volunteers."

—Whoopi Goldberg

Fundraisers Should Also Be Fun-Raisers

Although your primary concern is for your charitable project and those that it helps, you also need to focus on how to get the money to make your project happen. Fundraisers should be renamed fun-raisers because they serve two purposes: to raise money and to increase the bond among your members.

I will present tips and ideas for various fundraisers in this chapter. However, if you have a unique way of earning money for nonprofit organizations in your community, by all means, go for it. Be creative! If you see that there will be a major event in your town, such as a marathon or fair, set up a fundraising table at that event. Sell morning doughnuts, bagels, and juice. Sell lemonade or bottled water. Whatever you decide to sell, get permission from your township and develop a good budget to make sure you will realize a profit.

Fundraisers fall into two categories: direct sales and solicitation. *Direct sales* are a way to raise money where you offer goods in exchange for money that is donated to the organization. This type of fundraiser is common. For example, people expect and anticipate the local Girl Scouts to sell cookies each year. *Solicitation* involves requesting funds from individuals and companies for tax-deductible purposes. Direct sales are more fun and generate group enthusiasm. Solicitation, however, can sometimes raise the funds to cover your budget more rapidly.

Before you begin to sell anything, do a market analysis. What might your community need? What is already being sold in consignment shops or craft stores? What prices do those stores charge? The answers to these questions will help you identify a need, a market, and a price to charge for the items you sell.

Remember, whatever you decide to do as a fundraiser, it might be a good idea to plan ahead to do something different next year. That way, you tap into a different market and your members don't get bored. Consider this: If someone bought your flower magnets one year, they would be less likely to buy them again the next year. They would, however, be more likely to buy your handcrafted greeting cards.

Naturally, you could go with a commercial fundraising company and sell anything from cartoon character–shaped soaps to candy bars with your logo on them. In my experience, however, these campaigns tend to turn the children into little salespeople rather than junior philanthropists. Try to keep your members centered on their project, not on the way to make money to achieve their goals.

This chapter will give you ideas on how to raise money without signing a contract for 5,000 candy bars. They may be a little less profitable, but they're definitely more fun, engaging the youth in the planning process and getting your group's message to the community in a positive way. There are five basic reasons why fundraisers fail. David Westbrook researched these reasons and found that if a fundraiser is done improperly, it can actually have a negative effect on the effort and can cause the group to lose, rather than gain money. This is what he found, with my comments about how to avoid these failures in parentheses:

- Without a written plan, members wander aimlessly from idea to idea. (Develop a plan with specific goals, objectives, and a time line.)
- Sometimes fundraisers do not present an urgency to their appeal for funds. (Present this message: "We must raise $500 by November 10 for supplies, so we can give the residents at St. Jude's Nursing Home their gift bags this year.")
- If a fundraiser isn't fun for the youth group members and the donors, you won't get repeat business the following year. (Try a Roman chariot wash, where your members dress in togas . . . over their shorts and T-shirts, of course . . . as they wash cars.)
- Last-minute planning leads to last-minute failure. (Begin planning for your spring fundraiser in the fall.)
- Fund raisers can't be too shy to ask for the money. (Help your young members be assertive by having them present their need, and then say, "Would you like to donate?" Caution: Some people are offended when you ask them "how much" they would like to donate. Having children practice on other group members beforehand will help them gain confidence.)

Craft Shows

The most successful craft shows generally are based around a theme. Naturally, an easy theme is Christmas. Make ornaments, put up a tree, charge

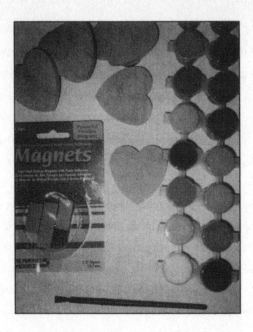

a set amount for each ornament, and count your money at the end of the day. This is a simple, neat, and effective approach.

A little more creativity, however, may reap more profits. If your crafts are related to your project, remember to ask your members to create posters and brochures that use both pictures and words to advertise their project. Placing them at your table should increase sales. Make sure there are plenty of bags available and that you have a supply of cash receipts on hand for people who itemize their taxes. The cash receipt should have the name of your nonprofit organization at the top, the amount received and from whom, then a place for your (always an adult) signature. Consider craft tables with the following themes, which could be related to your project:

- *Children of the World:* Play "It's a Small World" at your table; create things kids will enjoy—simple toys and games. (For your project that helps children.)

- *Animal Kingdom:* Set up a small television playing a video or DVD about animals, create greeting cards with animals on them, sell hand-made birdhouses or items made from shells. (For your project that helps animals.)
- *Angels:* Use a lit Christmas tree top as a centerpiece. Create angel ornaments, angel sun catchers, and angel cards. (Buyers will become angels for helping the homeless, handicapped, senior citizens, or the hospitalized.)
- *All-American:* Naturally, the centerpiece will be an American flag. Sell flags, flag pins, patriotic ornaments, and anything red, white, and blue. (For your project that supports military personnel and American history or restoration.)
- *Green Thumb:* Have a showpiece flower in the center. For that center-piece, either write "not for sale" on it or raffle it as part of your fundraiser. Sell flowers that the members have raised from seed. You can also sell growing kits that consist of seeds, a resealable plastic bag of potting soil, and a small clay pot. (For your project that cleans up urban eyesores.)

These are not all the themes that you could use; they are merely here to jog your imagination. What do they all have in common? They use an attention-attracting device, such as a tape, video, or centerpiece, and they sell related items. When you draw people to your table from a sea of other tables by setting yourself apart from the competition, you will be more profitable. How else can you increase your profit margin?

- Set reasonable prices for your products. Most people go to craft fairs expecting to spend between $2 and $10 per item. Make sure the prices are clearly marked. If people have to ask the price, they will usually pass by and go to the next table.

- Offer gift wrapping for an additional small charge. This small effort can set your table apart from the other craft tables and it gets more of your members involved in the effort.
- Set up an attractive display: Group items of the same color or purpose, use a tablecloth over the standard table, add lights—either battery-operated or plug-in if an outlet is available, play music, dress in costume (if appropriate). Definitely have a centerpiece that is related to your theme or project.
- Near the brochure that describes your project, place a donation can for people who just want to donate and don't need what you're selling.
- In addition to selling your handmade crafts, have a tray of wrapped cookies or brownies that will sell for a low price. Again, this attracts those who want to help, don't want crafts, but do want something for their money.

Dorise Salado shows off the quilt she made.

Participating in one or more craft shows throughout the year accomplishes two purposes: it allows you to add to your revenue and it also is free publicity for your project, which could bring in more group members and donors.

If you and your members are especially energetic and organized, you can hold your own craft fair, charging for tables and arranging for the publicity. It's a lot of work, but it could also generate a lot of revenue.

Car Wash

The first rule for car washes is: always have them in the spring. This is the time of year when people are looking to get the winter grime and salt from their cars. What better way than to help the local youth trying to raise money for a good cause?

Car washes as fundraisers for teen youth groups are excellent ways to build community. The kids have fun with the water and earn money at the same time. There is little up-front expense involved and very little preparation. It is great for groups where the members have little talent for crafts. Make sure the place that you hold your car wash has an outdoor water supply and plenty of room for moving cars through without backing up traffic on the street. If you don't have ready access to a parking lot, remember that you can ask for permission to use a bank lot or the parking lot of another business closed on the day you want to have the car wash.

The key to a successful car wash is publicity. Follow these simple guidelines for a profitable fundraiser:

- Publicize your event with posters around the neighborhood. Make sure you list a rain date.
- On the day of your car wash, rotate the members through washing, drying, collecting money, and waving down customers. Have a

member hold a placard near your location that advertises your car wash. I've seen kids dressed in all sorts of Halloween costumes to draw attention to their car wash.

Garage Sales

What an awesome way to clean out the attic and basement while raising funds for your charitable project! There are only a few guidelines and precautions that I'll present, but this is one of the most profitable fundraisers and requires very little preparation. All of the members can participate in some way and everyone benefits.

The first decision regarding a garage sale is where to have it and when. You could have it at someone's home, the parking lot of your religious center, or at a community yard sale location. Try to have your sale before it gets too hot during the summer and after the spring rainy season ends. The end of June is a very good time. It's after exams and before the vacation season truly begins. However, if you think your members would like to work on cleaning out their basements and attics during summer vacation, then by all means hold a yard sale in August or September. But remember that there are several disadvantages with a late summer sale. People may already have been to many yard sales throughout the summer and may have found all the slightly used items they need. Also, once school starts, the sports season also begins, which will take time from your students for their fundraising efforts.

Beware of local ordinances. Some townships require a permit that you must obtain at least a month before your scheduled yard sale. Other townships have limits on the number of sales an individual or group can have. Make sure you know your township's laws before proceeding with plans.

As with craft shows, you can increase your profit margin with garage sales by selling baked goods and having a donation can near your flyers. Remember to mark each item clearly and tell your members to be prepared for haggling. Part of the appeal of yard sales is that the patrons enjoy getting a bargain, even if that means you will sell an old sconce for one dollar instead of two.

You might also consider the online garage sale as a way to get money for your charitable project. List your items on eBay for a reasonable price, checking to see what similar items sold for. At the end of the sale, have your members wrap, address, and send them. For your convenience, set up a PayPal account for the group so that all the money received will go directly there. Remember to reimburse your members for postage because it will be included in the price of the merchandise sold. Items that are not sold on eBay could then be sold at a local yard sale.

EBay also has a "Giving Works" program through which the money earned from your sale goes directly to the charity of your choice. That's not as much fun as standing in the sun to sell your items at a yard sale and then using those funds to make door decorations for senior citizens in nursing homes. It is, however, a very easy way to donate money to major charitable organizations, such as Habitat for Humanity. For more information, go directly to www.ebay.com/givingworks. You'll find ideas on how to use their Web site to earn money for your own project and for larger organizations.

Raffles

Be careful! Raffles and bingos carry many different rules and requirements depending on your state. In some states, you need to register with the Legalized Games of Chance Control Commission in order to raffle something that benefits a nonprofit organization. Whether you're raffling off a quilt or a car, the necessary paperwork must be completed and approved well in advance of when you begin to sell tickets.

You also may be required to register as a tax-exempt organization, which involves filing regular reports. Only religious organizations and schools that file their curricula with the Department of Education are exempt from the provisions of the Charitable Registration and Investigation Act. In some states, only a nonprofit that raises less than $10,000 is exempt from the application fee.

If you are part of a larger group, such as the Girl Scouts or YMCA, you don't need to worry about filing status. Simply check with the central office regarding raffles. If you're not sure whether you need to file with your state, I strongly recommend that you call or email them with your information before you proceed with any games of chance.

For the most part, if the participants will only be your members or their families, and the raffle is for fun and a small profit, then you probably don't need to register. For example, if your group wants to raffle a quilt made by someone's mother and the tickets say "donation" rather than "fee," and you request "donations" from friends and family, you're pretty safe. However, if you raffle that same quilt at your craft show table where the general public will be giving "donations," then it's another story. As I said before, check with your state to review the guidelines for raffles.

So, let's assume that you have secured the necessary approvals, you have your quilt ready to raffle, and you have even gotten a sponsor to print the tickets, what's next?

I recommend that you get press coverage for your raffle to assure credibility. That way, nobody can say that you fixed the raffle so a specific person can win it. Also, it's a good idea to have a representative from the group that you will be assisting with the proceeds to pick the winning ticket. I'll finish this section on raffles with a reminder: be careful!

Chinese Auctions

Chinese auctions probably did not originate in China. Some people think that the name is a corruption of "chance auction." Unlike traditional auctions where people bid to buy merchandise, Chinese auctions are a combination of a raffle and an auction. They can be very profitable for charitable organizations, and most states do not require a special permit to hold a Chinese auction.

In a Chinese auction, people buy a strip of numbered tickets for a set price. They keep one half of the ticket and place the matching half in a collection cup associated with a prize. During the "auction," someone pulls the winning ticket from each cup. In addition to the pulling of prize tickets, a Chinese auction usually has refreshments and may also have entertainment. Here are some tips for a successful Chinese auction:

- Advertise about a month in advance of your event to give people plenty of time to plan for it.
- Ticket sales may be done in one of two ways: either sell strips of tickets, which means that people need to remember many numbers, or sell a card of tickets that has the same number on each ticket plus a marker ticket that records the number. You can preprint the cards or have them professionally printed. Either way, you could solicit a donation from a local company that would get a printed advertisement on the marker ticket that your patrons retain during the auction.
- The best Chinese auctions have many prizes. Go around to local businesses to get gift certificates and donated items. Ask for donations from your youth group members and their families.
- A tray/basket party is a variation on the traditional theme. Assemble at least 50 baskets or trays with related contents. Wrap in cellophane and tie with a bow. Patrons place tickets in a cup near the basket or tray they would like to win. Examples of basket contents are things for sports enthusiasts, writers, readers, and puzzlers in addition to baskets that contain items for bath, kitchen, or barbecue. Don't forget to have baskets with toys for the kids—some for girls, some for boys, and

some for either. The basket auction works well if you have so many prizes that you need three hours to announce all the winners!

- Make sure the cups for tickets are numbered to match prizes so people know which cup goes with which prize.

- Have more than enough refreshments—cookies, cupcakes, brownies, cheese and crackers, coffee, and soda or punch with ice. Remember to include plates, cups, and napkins.

- Enlist the help of an outgoing person to be your emcee. An announcer who makes people laugh as they watch someone else win a prize they wanted is valuable to the success of your auction. He or she will encourage people to return to your Chinese auction next year.

- How much should you charge for your tickets? A common price is three tickets for $1.00 or $10.00 for a card of 20 preprinted tickets. However, don't mix and match the two types of tickets.

Bake Sales

Bake sales are a nice, safe way to earn money on a regular basis. Many youth groups have bake sales at their church, temple, or school every month. It's one of the few moneymaking events that can be repeated without having your patrons become bored with the same products. In fact, many people look forward to those same old products, especially if those products are delicious.

For safety, baked goods should only be unrefrigerated for an hour at most. If your sale goes longer than that, arrange for refrigeration and transfer the baked goods to the sale table as the supply dwindles. Also, make sure that they are wrapped in clear plastic for health reasons.

Here are some tips for bake sale success, in addition to having delicious items:

- If your organization has been holding bake sales for a while, you could take advance orders for the next sale. Include advance sale slips on your publicity flier. Have the patron write her name, phone number, and requested baked item. Mark on that slip the guaranteed price for her purchase. Shortly before the sale, call to make sure she is still interested.

- Publicize home delivery of your baked goods to those unable to get to your bake sale.
- Remember themes for the craft show? They work equally well for bake sales. Have a tablecloth and centerpiece that express your theme. If you use the same themed tablecloth each time because it goes with your charitable project, put a sheet of plastic over the tablecloth to protect it from crumbs.
- Make sure you post a sign that includes the name of your organization and the project that your bake sale supports. Add flyers and a donation can, as well.
- Include a folded thank-you note on each baked item. The top could be for the price and description of the product. Inside you would write "Thanks for supporting the East Ambler Youth Group" (inserting the name of your group instead).
- Include items with a variety of prices. That means you should have everything from entire cakes to plates of brownies and small bags of cookies.
- Make your food pretty: Dip cookies in chocolate, add sprinkles to cupcakes, and drizzle icing onto bundt cakes.
- Have a variety of flavors, such as applesauce cake, banana muffins, and chocolate cookies. Get creative with their names: you'll be able to charge a higher price for "Granny's Applesauce Cake," "Tropical Banana Muffins," and "Decadent Chocolate Cookies."
- Clearly mark items that contain chocolate, nuts, and seeds for those who are allergic.
- Make sure you have plenty of cash for change.
- Be professional and have your members wear aprons while they sell.

- Find a business that would be willing to match the funds you raise during your sale. It's a tax-deductible donation for them and it doubles the income for you. Advertise this on a sign at your table. You may be pleasantly surprised with the results.
- Location, location, location. Arrange to have your bake sale somewhere that attracts many people, such as at a church after services or at the local grocery store on a Saturday morning.
- Publicize, publicize, publicize. Print fliers and posters. Place them around town and where you will be having the sale. Most good bake sales fail for lack of adequate publicity.

Gift Wrapping Service

When churches have Christmas bazaars, your youth group could earn some extra money by having a gift-wrapping booth. Plan your budget well before setting prices. Figure how many shirt boxes you can wrap with a piece of paper, note how much the paper is, then adjust the price for a profit. Have those boxes handy, but charge an additional fee for them. You can also charge an additional fee for bows. Tags should be included with the price of the wrapping. Clearly mark your prices on a poster board. As an alternative to set prices, you could request donations. You might be surprised at how much you make.

Here's something you may not have considered: many children don't know how to wrap! You may need to hold an internal wrapping party before your fundraiser so the members are proficient. Show them how to create crisp corners and curl ribbon. Appoint the group member with the best handwriting to write the names on the tags.

You could even have several grades of paper. A simple box with curly ribbon and a tag might go for $2.00, while the same box in foil wrap with a professional bow would be $2.50. Know your audience. If you think there are people who would be willing to pay the higher price for better wrapping then by all means, offer it.

Remember to buy different styles of wrapping paper, curly ribbon, bows, tape, and tags in a quantity that will allow several of your members to wrap presents at the same time.

Discount Cards

In recent years, some organizations have solicited companies for support by getting them to agree to a percentage discount when your discount card is presented. My local high school's band sells these every year to support their trips. The card costs me $10 and gives me discounts at local auto repair shops, restaurants, and grocery stores.

If you decide to go with this type of fundraiser, make sure no other group in your area is also offering discount cards. It will be counterproductive for both organizations. Remember that you will need to pay the discount card provider for their printing services. This type of fundraiser is usually better for larger groups. For more information and links to card suppliers, go to www.fundraiserhelp.com/fundraising-discount-cards.htm.

_____-a-thons

Youth groups attempt to raise money for themselves and other nonprofit organizations by many forms of _____-a-thons. Some support the March of Dimes and participate in the annual Walk-a-thon, while others have internal fundraisers and sponsor Bike-a-thons, Bowl-a-thons, or Rock-a-thons (picture 20 or so rocking chairs going nonstop).

Organization of any _____-a-thon is easy. You simply print out pledge sheets for the participants to use. Include these columns on your pledge sheets for patrons to insert their information: Name, address, phone, $ pledged per _____, and $ donated. The last two columns are important because some people like to sponsor kids by the mile, book, and so forth, while other people like to donate a flat amount. After you have duplicated your pledge sheets, your young philanthropists can ask parents, grandparents, other relatives, friends, friends' parents, teachers, and neighbors to support their effort. Most people will donate a set amount, while others will buy into the _____-a-thon and pledge 10 cents a mile, 10 cents a bowling pin, or 10 cents an hour of rocking. After the _____-a-thon is over, the members go back to those who pledged and collect the money. Depending on how assertive your members are, you could raise between $100 and $10,000 for a successful _____-a–thon. You might also consider an Awake-a-thon. Members get donations for the number of hours that they can stay awake from 9:00 P.M. to 7:00 A.M. Your members probably won't get much sleep, but they'll have fun while they earn money for their projects. Also, remember that you will need adult chaperones or leaders for your _____-a-thons.

For any _____-a-thon, invite your patrons to come watch the kids bike, walk, run, or stay awake. This helps to authenticate the diligence of the members involved in the fundraiser. Write up a summary of what happened while the kids did their fundraiser, including funny incidents and where the donations will be used. The kids can then hand that to the supporter with the amount donated on it. This becomes a written record of the fundraiser and a tax-deductible receipt for the supporter.

Direct Donations

It is certainly possible that you could go directly to area businesses, tell them about your philanthropic project, and see if they want to subsidize your efforts in exchange for a tax deduction. This involves very little work except some phone calls or letters and preparation of receipts. However, it usually gives the children very little control over their project. When giving direct donations, corporate representatives prefer contacts from adults. So, if you want to focus more on getting money for your charitable project than on getting the children to work together for the total project, then go ahead and contact the companies in your area. You should realize, though, that they are sometimes inundated with similar requests. To set your group apart from others, follow these guidelines for preparing your request:

- Create a portfolio that has a professional appearance. List the goals and objectives for your project.
- Prepare a detailed description of your project, telling how the money will be spent and how it would benefit the community.
- Most companies will cooperate if they know that their funds will provide publicity. Promise that you will prominently display your donors' names in literature.
- Provide a detailed budget and promise an accounting of the monies spent when the project is done. Some things to consider in addition to supplies: camera, film, transportation, and overhead such as postage.
- If this is not the first year for your children to do a charitable project, enclose pictures of your members doing previous projects.
- Remember to include the name of your group, the logo, mission statement, and number of members with a contact name, phone number, and e-mail address.
- I'm sure this goes without saying, but it's so important that I'll write it again. Never, ever allow children to go door-to-door for direct donations without adult supervision.

Grants

Applying for grants is very similar to soliciting direct donations from a company, with one exception: be very careful to follow the guidelines set by the foundation or your grant will be rejected before it is even considered. Grants are available from small groups, such as the local PTA, to large corporations, such as American Eagle Outfitters. When you prepare your proposal, make sure you answer these questions somewhere in the application package:

- Why is this project necessary?
- How is it different from similar projects in the area?
- Why do you need to ask for financial aid?
- What research have you done to support the need? (Statistics are wonderful additions to any application.)
- What previous experience do you or anyone in your group have with your specific project or managing grants?
- When will you produce and publish results?

A grant application that is neat, organized, and supports a true community need is more likely to get the funding than an application that simply asks for a few thousand dollars to fix up the local park.

I can't emphasize enough how important it is to research the grantor's organization before writing your proposal. Read their mission statement and include reworded passages from it to support your proposal. Find out what they have funded previously and link your project to that project. Make sure that your project falls under their guidelines. For example, if a grant-making organization wants to support ecological projects, don't ask them for money to buy more books for the children's section of the library. Also, see what they typically support. Most organizations like to provide funds for supplies, equipment, transportation, and incidentals. They seldom fund salaries. Above all, make sure you meet the deadline for application.

Another problem with some grant applications is poor writing. You must have a good command of the English language in order to write a competitive proposal. Use correct spelling and punctuation. Avoid slang, long sentences, repetitious requests, and passive voice. Passive voice is a biggie. When a grantor reads, "We are attempting to correct the problem of senior citizens who have no relatives in the area," he or she will likely go on to the next application. On the other hand, if you are more positive and more active in your writing by saying, "We will provide assistance to senior citizens who have no immediate family in the area by creating an Adopt-a-Grandparent program," your application will proceed to the next stage, which will probably be a financial analysis.

Type your application in Times New Roman, 12-point type, on plain white paper. Don't use cute pink paper, an elaborate letterhead, or difficult-to-read typeface. Have the usual margins set by your word processing software. In other words, be professional, be concise, and be neat.

You should also know that local applications are rarely accepted by national organizations. There are a few exceptions. Some national companies will support local efforts in communities that are served by their stores. Best Buy, Wal-Mart, and American Eagle Outfitters are only three examples of those kinds of companies that you might tap for funds.

Here are examples of ways American Eagle Outfitters can offer financial assistance for your charitable project in areas served by their stores. American Eagle has discounted gift cards available that your group can sell. The difference between what you pay and what your patrons pay goes directly into your treasury for your project. American Eagle also provides grants. Below are their guidelines with my comments in parentheses.

- The organization and/or its programs must fall within the scope of the American Eagle Foundation's mission statement. (Every foundation has a mission statement and it is usually available online at the corporate Web site. American Eagle supports four initiatives according to its mission statement: To foster civic engagement, render a safe and nourishing place for teens, embrace diversity, and encourage youth/teen development. Pick one that supports your goals.)

- The organization must creatively involve American Eagle business unit and/or employees in projects. (Now there's a requirement you don't see often. Your project should be one that creatively enlists the aid of American Eagle employees or the store. So, if your group wants to supply gift bags to servicemen overseas, you could write a grant that uses American Eagle funds to buy the items and American Eagle employees to help work with your members to package and mail the gift bags.)
- The organization must provide regular reports of financial and program activities. (No surprises here. They just want to know how their money is spent. All foundations require that, so keep good records.)
- The organization must direct at least 70 percent of the money raised toward beneficiaries. (This means that only 30 percent can be used for the administrative costs of your project. For the sample military gift bags grant above, you can only allot 30 percent for postage, transportation, and incidentals.)
- The organization must be willing to provide documentation to American Eagle verifying financial donations. (Keep all of your receipts!)
- The organization or its program must be in a community where American Eagle operates business. (If you are unsure if your community is close enough to a store to qualify for the grant, contact American Eagle for clarification.)
- Preference will be given to proposals with multi-state or national scope or to organizations located in southwestern Pennsylvania, New York City, or eastern Kansas. (Although preference will be given to these areas, that doesn't mean that your group in New Mexico can't apply. It just means that you should apply with an outstanding project serving your community in an exceptional way.)
- Grant request should fall within $1,000 to $25,000 range. (Your project should be big enough that it needs at least $1,000 to fund. $25,000 is a lot of money to account for and spend, but I've written,

won, and implemented a grant [not from American Eagle] that came close to that amount for my school district.)

- The program/goal of the financial donation must significantly affect the surrounding community. (Remember our sample grant for the military—they would reject it because of this requirement. Instead, you might write a grant to provide a youth center for weekend activities that keeps teenagers busy.)

- The organization must be inclusive in policies and practices involving all genders, races, ages, ethnic origin, sexual orientation, or creed. (Obviously, you can't discriminate for or against any group that you serve.)

- If your organization meets all of the above criteria, you must submit a two-page overview. (The required information to be included in the overview can be found at their Web site and concerns the target population, description of the project, and how American Eagle is involved. You only have two pages to tell how your program is superior to other similar programs and how you will spend your money. Since they only ask for two pages, don't submit a detailed financial plan. Simply tell them that you will spend your money on lumber, building supplies, and so forth.)

- Attach a copy of the current IRS determination letter indicating a 501(c)(3) tax-exempt status, statement verifying payroll tax payments, list of officers and directors, current board-approved annual operating budget, including expense and earned income, and your most recent audited financial statements and IRS 990 forms. (At the very least, you must have a 501(c)(3) tax-exempt status prior to applying for the grant. However, if you have no paid employees or have never had your books audited, contact American Eagle to see if your group is eligible to apply.)

Finally, watch deadlines. American Eagle has rolling deadlines and awards grants at their quarterly board meetings. Other foundations have specific deadlines for annual applications. To search for one that is right for your group, go to http://fdncenter.org/. (See the Resources section for Web sites for other granting organizations and businesses.)

Other Fundraisers

Here is a list of other ways to raise money. I offer no suggestions for their implementation, simply a spark for your imagination.

- Challenge another youth group to a competition.
- Hold a spaghetti dinner.
- Provide Halloween insurance (stand outside the buyer's door to protect against tricks).
- Sell box lunches/dinners after religious services.
- Vote for your favorite . . . (Have pictures of local celebrities—such as the mayor, principal, and so forth—on plastic jugs. People would "vote" for their favorite by dropping money in the jug.)
- "Open" your own bank (Jewish tradition of tzadakah).
- Have a Kiddie Karnival.
- Hold a dance.
- Have a volleyball tournament.

Anything can be a fundraiser. Identify a need in your community, and then find a fun, safe, easy way to fulfill that need. The community benefits and the young participants will learn the value of helping others through an organized effort.

Advertising and Promotion

Advertising and promotion are the keys to making your fundraiser earn as much as possible. The key to a successful sale is to get the message out to your potential customers that you are having a sales campaign and what it is for.

Let's face it—most campaigns consist of posters and fliers. Unless you are going to buy billboard space or time on the radio, most of your efforts will be spent creating an attractive presentation on a piece of paper.

What aspects of posters make them appealing? Using a fundraiser that sells handmade animal magnets to benefit a local animal shelter as an example, consider these points.

- Your biggest letters should be the most important: Please help us!
- Below the heading, add your additional information: "Kids for Pups" is a group of students from Central Elementary School. We want to help provide food, shelter, and vaccines for the puppies at the East Ridge Animal Shelter. (If you have plenty of workers who made plenty of magnets, consider selling them at three for $2.00 to increase profits.)
- Use pictures that are large enough to see from a distance. Use pictures of two animals at the shelter to balance the poster. If they don't already have names, give them names below the picture.
- Use only two or three colors. For this poster, use earthy colors— ambers, greens, and browns. If you are creating a flier, use only two or three fonts.
- Posters don't need to be square. Paw print shape, perhaps?
- Slogans and logos increase interest in the poster: Show a little L♥VE. Adopt a pet or support our fundraiser.
- Tell when and where your products will be available and always include an adult's name and contact number. Sale day: October 10,

PLEASE HELP US!

"Kids for Pups" is a group of students from Central Elementary School. We want to help provide food, shelter, and vaccines for the puppies at the East Ridge Animal Shelter.

Refrigerator Magnets
$1.00 each
or
3 for $2.00

*Show a little L♥VE.
Adopt a pet or support
our fundraiser.*

"Spanky" and Kids for Pups thank you for your support.

Sale day: October 10, 10AM–4PM at the Fall Fun Festival in Freedom Park. Call Debbie at 555-1712 for more information.

10 A.M. to 4 P.M. at the Fall Fun Festival in Freedom Park. Call Debbie at 555-1712 for more information.

- Always remember to thank your supporters: Spanky and Kids for Pups thank you for your support.

Newsletters

Here's a little-known fact about newsletters: people don't read them unless there is a picture with nearly every article. So take digital pictures of your members in action—at meetings, fundraisers, and while doing activities associated with your philanthropic project. Embed those pictures in your text.

Newsletters generate interest in the project and help the general public understand your goals. They can help bring in more money and more members. However, done poorly, they may have the opposite effect.

To have a successful newsletter that accomplishes your purposes, keep these guidelines in mind:

- Keep the articles short and succinct.
- Publish only one or two pages once a month, once every other month, or quarterly.
- Solicit advertisers to help pay for overhead costs of printing and distribution.
- Use an easy-to-read font, such as Times New Roman.
- Print on both sides of the paper.
- Distribute only to your target audience—parents, community members, religious groups, and so forth.
- For a professional appearance, use newsletter software, such as Aldus PageMaker or MS Publisher. (Check with your local schools. Most already have these in place for student use.)

- Investigate the cost-effectiveness of professional printing, such as the low-cost online services provided at www.vistaprint.com.
- Check and double-check the spelling, punctuation, and grammar of your youthful writers. Always include bylines to credit your authors.
- In each newsletter, plan ahead and always include a lead to an article in the next issue.
- Place your most important article in the most prominent location—center front.
- Include information about your members, perhaps a spotlight article on a different member or her project each month.

Newsletters have the added effect of teaching journalism skills. The young people learn how to write to an audience, which is generally on their standardized tests, while they publicize their philanthropic project.

Other Publicity Ideas

You are limited only by your own creativity when it comes to publicity for your group or your fundraiser. I have seen some groups successfully add fliers to grocery bags. Others have had grocery bags printed with their message. If you have a print shop in your local school, consider asking them to print bumper stickers for your distribution. Perhaps someone in your group has a relative who owns an embroidery sewing machine. If so, you could design your own logo or message, then sew it onto shirts. If you want to use professionally personalized merchandise, go to www.cafepress.com. There you can create your own shirts, backpacks, bumper stickers, and more.

Two energetic endeavors include producing a video or play that advertises your fundraiser. The video might be played on your school's television production. The play could be performed at your church. Both involve much work that might otherwise be expended on your charitable projects or actual fundraiser. However, if your members want to do that, then go for it!

Bookkeeping

You've planned your project, held your fundraiser, and helped some needy cause. Do you truly know how successful you were? You will if you keep a record of all your expenses and outlay of time and money. This is required if you apply for a grant or belong to a larger organization; it is recommended for all groups to justify the time and effort you invest in your project. This will not only help you figure out how much money you raised on your project, but might also help you decide whether to repeat the steps for a second round of fundraising with the same project or inspire your group to try something new.

Here are guidelines for keeping financial records:

- Keep a record of funds that are taken in by noting the date, name of donor, and amount.
- Keep a record of funds expended by noting the date, purpose, amount, and who received the payment. You should also note which adult approved the expenditure.
- Maintain a running total of all money in and out of your treasury so you know how much you have at all times. If you have a member with computer skills, you can use software, such as Quicken, to streamline your accounting. It is relatively easy to use and some high schools offer courses to help students understand it.
- Never keep cash to pay bills. Deposit cash with your checks at all times, noting the source of the cash. Example: $30 for dues from Jefferson, Albright, and Jensch ($10 each).

- Provide receipts for all money received and retain a duplicate copy for your own records.
- You may need, or decide to establish, a voucher form for money expended. This requires group leaders to approve payments that leave the treasury.
- Keep a separate account of money received and spent for specific purposes, such as charitable projects, dues, and more. (This would be in addition to the regular treasury and is for information only.)
- An adult who was designated by the bank must sign checks.
- Pay bills promptly.
- Deposit funds regularly.

In addition to the financial bookkeeping, make sure you keep a record of time volunteered by each member. This helps you to see who is doing how much of the work, so you can urge reluctant members to participate. You should also formally evaluate the success of your project and accompanying fundraiser. This helps you eliminate the problems you encountered with previous projects. A sample evaluation form to assess a philanthropic project is included in the Evaluation Information section of this book (see page 145).

Part II

Get Real: Real Stories from Real People Doing Real Projects

Do you want to know what other youth leaders around the country are doing? In this section, you will meet adults, young adults, and children who are making a difference in the world. Read about successful leaders who help children engage in philanthropic pursuits. Learn how truly dedicated young people see a need and then develop the resources to fill that need. Their enthusiasm and success will spark your group into action. Then try one or more of these projects with your own group. These are the stories of real people doing real projects for real causes, just like you.

5

Real Interviews with Real Adults Who Help Real Youth with Philanthropic Projects

"When people volunteer, good things happen—those who receive the services are helped, those who provide the services are bettered, and our communities are enriched."

—Robert K. Goodwin, president and CEO
of the Points of Light Foundation

Meet a church leader who brought life into a failing youth group through her strong organizational skills and intuition, and generated teen motivation. See how a substance abuse coordinator rallies an entire high school to combat drug abuse with philanthropy. Then learn how a military wife and mother of three helps her children understand the value of kindness to others.

Lynette and her son Ryan, a member of F.L.I.G.H.T., begin preparations for the annual dinner at Ronald McDonald House.

Spotlight on: Lynette DeTata, A New Youth Group Leader

Service Projects Discussed: Thanksgiving dinners for the poor, Souper Bowl
   of Caring, dinner at Ronald McDonald House
Fundraiser Discussed: Gift wrap service

When you start a new youth group, you may find the task to be overwhelming at first. However, the youthful enthusiasm of your members carries you through the difficult first few months. This is what Lynette DeTata found as she rejuvenated the youth group at Holy Eucharist Catholic Church in Tabernacle, New Jersey. I (RH) interviewed DeTata (LD) recently and this is her story of how she established F.L.I.G.H.T. (Finding Light in God, Holy Eucharist Teens).

RH: Why do you think the youth group fell apart over the past few years?

LD: The previous leaders had an erratic meeting schedule. Some would meet monthly and others would meet every two weeks. The problem was that when holidays fell on the meeting week, there could be anywhere between three weeks and two months between meetings. Teens need consistency, so I decided to have meetings every Sunday night in a church meeting room at 7:00 P.M., a time that usually does not conflict with sports schedules and family obligations. Even with that regular schedule, there were times when the meeting was preempted by special circumstances. You also need to constantly stay in contact with the members. I made announcements in church, e-mailed them once a week, sent them written bulletins, posted notices on the church bulletin board, and updated the group's Web site. I use the Web site for many purposes, including posting meeting dates, making available an application form for new members, and providing a link to our monthly newsletter.

RH: What kinds of charitable projects were your members interested in doing?

LD: At first, they were all over the place with their ideas because service to others was their primary reason for joining. It was reassuring to see that they were eager to help. I felt it was necessary to focus on two or three special projects during that first year, so they would not burn out. They were especially interested in Habitat for Humanity, probably because it has had a lot of exposure on the news. (Habitat for Humanity International is a nonprofit, nondenominational Christian housing organization that has provided shelter for more than one million people since 1976.) After Hurricane Katrina, everyone was ready to hop on a bus bound for New Orleans to help Habitat for Humanity rebuild the area. However, Habitat has a requirement that none of their workers could be under the age of sixteen. Most members of my group were fourteen and fifteen years old.

After much discussion, we settled on three projects, spread out through the year. We began by helping our church collect and organize Thanksgiving dinners to those served by our St. Vincent DePaul Society. We did not help distribute the food to protect the identity of the recipients.

In January, we participated in the Souper Bowl of Caring, which is a national effort to inspire and mobilize youth to fight hunger and poverty on Super Bowl Sunday. The youth group members stood at the doors and asked for donations after Mass. The $370 that we collected went directly to our own St. Vincent DePaul Society to help them with food distribution through the rest of the year.

Our third project was a major effort. I'm glad we did this at the end of our first year, so we would be more organized. We brought dinner to a local Ronald McDonald House on Sunday evening in place of our regular meeting. We cooked the food at my house, transported it to the Ronald McDonald House, and set up the buffet table for the families who were there at the time. We made a pork roast, rice, peas and onions, and three cakes. We also purchased applesauce, salad, and bread. The cooking effort only took about two hours. because we made all the other food while the pork was in the oven. We left Ronald McDonald House after we set up the buffet table because it was getting late, so my only regret was that there was not much interaction between our group members and the families there.

RH: What fundraisers did you have to support your charitable projects?

LD: We held bake sales and bagel sales after church. We also ran a gift-wrap service for two weekends in December. The kids chose the gift wrap and tags; Wal-Mart donated the bows. We advertised the service in our church bulletin. People dropped off their bags of gifts that they had marked with their name and the name of the recipients. Then they came back a few hours later to pick up their wrapped presents. We asked only for a donation, and the parishioners were very generous. We found it easier than posting prices per item. We had a lot of materials left over, so next year, the donations will be all profit. The best part of the wrapping service was the camaraderie formed by the youth group members. Remember, this was the first year we had been together, so we were still getting to know each other. With Christmas carols in the background, and plenty of doughnuts and cocoa for the hungry teens, I think we raised as much fun as money.

RH: It sounds like you have revitalized the youth group very nicely. Do you have any other adults helping you?

LD: No. By the time children reach high school, most parents are done with the room-parent routine. Also, it's a sad, but true comment that many adults are fearful of working with teenagers. They think they are all on drugs, carry knives, and have aggressive tendencies. I think the reverse is true. The young adults in my youth group are wonderful individuals and I am thankful every day to have met them. But that doesn't solve the problem that I was the only adult with 15 to 20 teenagers. I would have liked at least one, perhaps two other adults, who could have led small group discussions during our weekly meetings. I have one volunteer who said she would help next year during meetings when I know we will have small group discussions.

RH: What advice would you give to new youth group leaders?

LD: Go for training. Our diocese offered training sessions for new youth group leaders that were invaluable. I learned how to plan programs, recruit members, run small and large group discussions, and address teen problems. I also learned how to manage the legal aspects of leading a youth group, such as reporting abuse that may have come up during small group discussion. The 10 sessions prepared me to be certified as a youth minister.

I would also recommend that leaders know their limitations and not try to do too much the first year. Take baby steps and you will meet your goals. You also need to plan activities that are just plain fun—skating trips, pool parties, picnics, and softball games all bond the members so they can work together well when they do their charitable work. Finally, I would recommend that the youth group leader have a paid position. Although it's good to say that you're doing something to help the youth in your religious community, the truth is that being a youth leader involves a lot of work. I put in 25 hours a week sometimes, so the salary I receive helps me to stay focused on my "job" as youth group leader.

Author's Note: Lynette DeTata keeps a sign over her desk that reminds her of her goal for the group: "To help our youth to a stronger faith so that they can stay active in the church. That by their participation in our youth group they will learn they can turn to Christ and the church to answer questions and solve problems in their lives." Certainly, with her efforts, the youth of Holy Eucharist Parish are learning to become responsible adults who can turn to God for help with their problems.

Al Borris with his daughter, Alexandra, who is in ninth grade at Moorestown High School. While in seventh grade, she became the youngest cross-age teacher to work in the elementary schools.

Spotlight on: Al Borris, Substance Abuse Coordinator

Service Projects Discussed: Natural Helpers curriculum, environmental cleanup day, and sports teams volunteer effort
Fundraiser Discussed: Bake sale

Al Borris (AB) works with hundreds of students each day. Sometimes he works with them directly as the teacher of the Natural Helpers course at Moorestown High School in Moorestown, New Jersey. In his office, he might counsel a student who has become involved with illegal or harmful drugs. At other times, he works with the students indirectly by coordinating the service opportunities at the high school.

RH: Why is service learning important in a high school?

AB: When teens are involved in service, they are less likely to abuse drugs and alcohol. They are also more likely to become responsible leaders, both now and in the future. Service hours are not required at

Moorestown High School. Rather, the students are encouraged to perform service projects in their classes, their clubs, and their sports. Each teacher, leader, or coach helps the students to find ways that they can give hours to community service.

RH: Tell me about the Natural Helpers course that you teach.

AB: It is a human relations seminar that is designed to teach helping and negotiating skills to students. It is a semester course offered for 2.5 credits. The Natural Helpers curriculum focuses on topics of interest to teenagers, such as leadership development, personal improvement, drug and alcohol awareness, sexuality, and suicide. Students are made aware of community resources and agencies that help those in need. They take field trips to visit these agencies and are encouraged to participate in an optional retreat in early September. We watch movies and discuss the social issues involved. The students also learn about the Community Alliance on Substance Abuse. Last year, they volunteered at a sober Super Bowl party and participated in an all-night volleyball event to raise funds for Big Brothers/Big Sisters. Ultimately, the students in this class become resources and advocates for other students.

RH: That sounds like a valuable part of a student's education. What volunteering efforts have the students who are not enrolled in this course done?

AB: There are so many, but I'll mention just a few. The TeenAIDS task force organizes AIDS walks and provides HIV education. Many students volunteered their time during a community service day to clean up Pompeston Creek. Students needed to have a permission slip signed by a parent or guardian and bring a lunch. They took a bus from the high school to the creek, where they helped remove invasive plants and debris to beautify the area. This activity was both educational and service-oriented, as the students learned about watershed management while they improved the ecological health of the creek. Other students might participate in the Toys for Tots campaign, local soup kitchens, and clothing drives. Most recently, they participated in a bake sale to help the victims of Hurricane Katrina. We also have a very active Interact Club that works directly with the Moorestown Rotary to implement their projects.

RH: Do the students do any service projects for younger children in the elementary schools?

AB: Yes. The boys' basketball team holds a basketball clinic for elementary age children. We also have a Cross-Age Teachers (CATs) club. These members volunteer one day a week in the lower grades to tutor, help with homework, and read to the children. They may also help teachers grade papers or prepare special projects. These student volunteers work in grades K to 8 after school. Within our high school community, seniors participate in the Big Brothers/Big Sisters programs by mentoring freshmen and transfer students to ease the transition. They meet weekly for social functions, orientation, and tutoring, if needed. Our Challenge Club, which helps members stretch the limits of their physical endurance, assists with middle school rock climbing on Tuesday afternoons. They also organize Grandparents Unlimited to help senior citizens volunteer their time and talents in the schools and community.

RH: What advice would you give other counselors or teachers who want to begin a charitable giving campaign at their schools?

AB: Just start. Begin with one project, and then encourage others to do the same. Have more focus on the goal than the process at first. Start with a project that does not require much money or organization, perhaps a simple bake sale to benefit a local soup kitchen. Kids need things to do, and if those things that they do help someone else, then they are learning a valuable lesson in giving. At a faculty meeting, you could recommend that teachers include service learning as part of their curriculum or that club leaders and coaches include philanthropic projects in their yearly plan of activities. Keep your eyes and ears open for opportunities to help. Post notices on a bulletin board or develop a philanthropy newsletter. No matter what you do, big or small, involving money or not, if a young person helps someone else, he or she is also contributing to his or her own personal success.

Author's Note: On the day that I interviewed Borris, he appeared wearing a tuxedo. I asked him what the occasion was. He answered that all his suits were in the cleaners. He added, "I could either dress up or dress down, so I chose the high road because it gives me visibility in a positive way with the students."

Linda and her three children, Logan, Adam, and Erin, cut coupons for charity on Sunday afternoons.

Spotlight on: Linda Dawe, a busy mom who shows her children the value of philanthropy

Service Projects Discussed: Cutting coupons for charity, adopting a family at Christmas, supplies for homeless shelters, and Katrina relief effort
Fundraiser Discussed: Trash treasure hunting, "Giving" banks

With three small children and a military husband who is frequently sent overseas, Linda Dawe (LD) needed to find a way for her children to be busy and productive. She found that little philanthropic projects turned into a huge bonus because her children, she says, think of others before they think of themselves. She was eager to tell her story so that others may do similar projects with their children.

RH: Tell me about your family.

LD: I have three children. Adam is ten years old, Erin is nine, and Logan is seven. My husband, Scott, is in the Air Force. We look forward to our time together because he is deployed frequently.

RH: How did you get the idea to do charitable projects with your children to keep them busy?

LD: My mother was active in the church and when I was young, she encouraged me to help other people. She stressed giving as a way of life. She helped me to count my blessings. I willingly gave away the clothes that I had outgrown and helped out at our church whenever Mom went to volunteer her time. As I matured, I would volunteer time babysitting for families that didn't have much money. I'm trying to convey that sense of giving to my children. However, your readers should know that my children are also active in other ways. They play soccer and get very good grades in school. I think it is important that they have a well-rounded education that includes philanthropy.

RH: What kinds of charitable projects have you done with your children?

LD: When my children were very little, they could not make crafts for a craft show or earn money for an organization by running a marathon. They could, however, cut with scissors very well. So, we began cutting coupons from the newspaper. We use those coupons in two ways. First, if we participate in a buy one, get one free promotion, we donate the free item to charity. Then we also try to find out how cheaply we can buy something with coupons, so I am teaching my children basic economics. Sunday afternoons or evenings became our coupon days. We would cut and sort them into categories and this activity became a family bonding event.

Second, we look for free promotions that involve sending in UPC codes or box tops. Since we probably wouldn't eat fifteen boxes of cereal in a week, we began our "Treasure Hunts." This involves going out on recycling day to find the required part of a package to earn the promotion. We only participate in programs that do not require sending in a proof of purchase, obviously. My kids have come to look at it as a game.

They go from pile to pile, searching for the required items, and when they find them, they get all excited. I do the cutting and handling of the recycled items. Their job is search and rescue. Some people wonder why we go trash picking like that, but it is not a dirty job. Recycled paper is clean and you're supposed to rinse your cans and bottles before tossing them in the recycling buckets. We have found a lot of Campbell's products that way. My children's school does not need the labels because we get military impact aid from the government. So, we usually give the labels to a local private school. Once again, a charitable project also became a family bonding activity.

RH: I would have never thought to collect box tops curbside! What kinds of things did you earn?

LD: We have gotten miscellaneous things from CDs and DVDs to shirts and markers. But my favorite collection came one Christmas. Every year, we adopt a family who might not otherwise have presents under their tree. It's not always the same family, so we sometimes don't know what the children might need or want. One year, we got a family with three preteen boys who wanted skateboards. We found offers that earned us three Mongoose skateboards, warm knit hats, and gloves. The only thing we had to pay was $5.95 shipping for each skateboard. It showed my children that you don't have to be rich to give to someone else.

RH: That's an amazing story. Do you do any other projects that don't involve "treasure hunts"?

LD: Yes, we assemble backpacks and shoeboxes for homeless shelters. We find inexpensive items that might be needed in a shelter and put them into a shoebox or backpack. Sometimes, we earn those backpacks from our treasure hunts. We put in soaps, coloring books, crayons, and school supplies. Most of these things we get from redeeming coupons or at the dollar store. I think that the recipients of the boxes are very thankful that someone cares enough to put them together. I don't think they calculate how much the contents cost, so whatever we give is definitely appreciated.

RH: Hurricane Katrina recently hit the Gulf Coast. What has your family done to help the recovery efforts?

LD: Hurricane Katrina hit my family personally because my parents lived in New Orleans. For three days, we heard nothing from them. Finally, we got the call that they were safe with my sister in North Carolina. After that worry was over, we began to plan how we could help. My children all decided that the homeless children would need toys. So they went into their rooms and chose their own toys that had been gently used. They cleaned them and we brought them to a distribution point. It warmed my heart to see my children taking the initiative for their own charitable project.

RH: It looks like you have instilled a sense of giving in your children at an early age. What advice do you have for other parents?

LD: I think children instinctively want to help others. We parents need to be role models so they can develop that sense of giving. We need to provide opportunities for them to appreciate what they have and to give to those who are less fortunate. Teaching about charity is just as important as teaching good sportsmanship and study skills when you raise your children.

Author's Note: I have a friend who helps her children save their money for charitable projects. They have two piggy banks. One is labeled with the child's name and the other is labeled, "Giving Bank." When I asked Linda if she does this with her children, she replied, "We will as soon as I get home!"

6

Real Stories from Real Kids Doing Real Philanthropy

"My grandfather once told me that there were two kinds of people: those who do the work and those who take the credit. He told me to try to be in the first group; there was much less competition."

—Indira Gandhi

While researching the material for this book, I met some amazing young people who organized major philanthropic projects. Most have formed their own foundations. They target senior citizens, dogs, children, military families, and medical illnesses for their efforts. All expend enormous amounts of energy helping others. I hope you find these stories as inspiring as I do.

Julie, on the left, and Cara, on the right.

Spotlight on: Julie Miller

Service Projects Discussed: Drama troupe for deaf children, sign language education

Fundraiser Discussed: Performances for deaf and hearing audiences

When Julie Miller founded a drama club for both hearing and deaf students from three schools around her Connecticut hometown, it was simply one more step in her quest to bridge the gap between two cultures. At age 16 in 2005, she produced a children's show featuring both sign language and spoken voice.

Julie's motivation for this creative endeavor was her older sister, Cara, who was born deaf. "My sister missed out on many aspects of life that hearing people take advantage of," says Julie. "Growing up, I had seen her too many times feeling excluded and ashamed of her deafness." She recalls seeing her sister cry with frustration because she was unable to understand something. Although Julie helped her sister as much as she could, she felt it wasn't enough. She wanted to do more to include Cara and other deaf people in her area.

When she lived in Maryland, Julie was an actor in the drama troupe Deaf Access Company, a part of Imagination Stage, founded and directed by Lisa Agogliati. After she moved to Connecticut, she wanted to continue to prove that regardless of young people's ability to hear, they can have full access to theater. She wanted to bring the deaf and hearing communities together on her own in a new setting.

At first, Julie started sign language clubs at two high schools. She taught the members of the clubs how to sign, and then those members taught basic sign language to hearing preschoolers so they would be able to communicate with deaf children. Next, she contacted the American School for the Deaf in West Hartford Connecticut, the first residential deaf school in America, founded in 1817. She proposed combining the two high school sign language clubs with the existing drama club at the American School for the Deaf, creating a troupe of deaf, hearing, and hard-of-hearing teenagers, which Julie called "Hand-In-Hand."

Julie chose the script and music. Then she auditioned the prospective actors, made the costumes and scenery, directed rehearsals, raised over $1,500, and contacted local schools to schedule performances. Her immediate goal was to have deaf teenagers and hearing teenagers work together to show that, despite differences, everyone can work together to create something wonderful. She wanted to demonstrate that deaf people were no different from hearing people, except that they could not hear.

Julie's 2003 performance was called *Coyote and the Circle of Tales*, a production of four Native American folktales. Ultimately, the troupe gave seven performances for over 2,000 children in elementary school. In 2004, they performed *Tales from Around the World*, which was presented to 1,500 hearing children. She is looking for ways to expand her endeavor to include more actors and more performances. Julie says that her most rewarding memory from these performances is seeing hundreds of little hands shaking in the air (sign language for applause). "Just knowing that, someday, these kids will recall seeing my group makes all of the hard work well worth the effort," Julie commented.

Julie's performances also include dance and music. How can that be? She cranks the volume up so high that the hearing kids cover their ears, but the deaf kids can feel the vibrations through the floor.

Expanding her volunteer work with the deaf community, Julie traveled to Costa Rica in the summer of 2005, where she spent three weeks at the only deaf school in the country. There, she worked with five- and six-year-old children with profound hearing losses, assisting with educational activities and helping around the school. Julie also spoke to the parents of the deaf children at the school, sharing her experiences as the sister of a deaf adult, and giving them hope that, yes, their children can still flourish in a predominantly hearing world. Every day at the school, Julie spoke in Spanish and signed in LESCO, Costa Rican sign language—this meant that she was translating four languages simultaneously. Talk about multi-tasking!

Julie has lent her time and energy to many different populations throughout her young life. She established a reading program for homeless children, started a youth-volunteering initiative at a local Alzheimer's residential care facility, and brought sign language and drama to children in several residential mental health facilities. Julie has also enjoyed volunteering at camps and schools for mentally retarded and autistic children and teenagers, and, of course, schools for deaf children. While in Costa Rica, Julie also volunteered at an orphanage and a home for people with terminal HIV/AIDS.

In addition to the Presidential Service Award, an award given to Americans who have logged at least 4,000 hours of community service, Julie has earned a Prudential Spirit of Community Award, an annual national volunteering award given to the top high school and middle school volunteers from each state. She was also given a Daily Point of Light award for March 24, 2005, a national community service award established by former president George H. W. Bush honoring one volunteer per day. She was given the 2005 Alexander Hamilton Friends Association Award, a new award honoring the top 20 youth volunteers in the nation. According to Julie, "I never had any idea anything like this would be possible. I just wanted to see the deaf and the hearing collaborating and putting on a drama show."

Annie Wignall surrounded by her Care Bags.

Spotlight on: Annie Wignall

Service Project Discussed: Care bags for underprivileged children
Fundraiser Discussed: Direct donations

At 11 years old, Annie Wignall learned there were a lot of kids in crisis situations who had to leave their homes with very few of their own belongings. "I love kids and wanted to do something to help make their lives better," says the Iowa resident. What began as a small project in 2000 to help a few local children has blossomed into a national effort. Annie formed her own Care Bags Foundation, a legal, nonprofit 501(c)(3) charitable organization, with a mission statement: To provide Care Bags filled with new essential, helpful, fun, safe, and age-appropriate items for children/youth (ages baby to 18 years) who are in need.

What are Care Bags? They are hand-sewn fabric bags that hold items to comfort children. Every bag is different, but each bag has a poem attached to the outside of it to say she cares. It may include a stuffed animal, toiletries, comb, toothbrush, game, toys, a journal, or a book. Annie has posted a list of items that she likes to include at her Web site: www.carebags4kids.org. She will also send out a starter kit by e-mail if you would like to begin a similar project in your area. Annie distributes her bags through child-service agencies and caring individuals across the United States. She even has international partners who hand-deliver the Care Bags to displaced, abused, and disadvantaged kids worldwide.

Originally, Annie went to local stores asking for donations to fill her bags. As word of her philanthropic project spread, businesses, groups, and individuals of all ages from across America started to donate items and to sew bags for her project. Look at the donor list on her Web site and be amazed by how many people and corporations volunteer time, donate new items, or contribute money to the Care Bags Foundation. With their help, Annie has already brought smiles to the faces of more than 8,000 deserving kids around the world.

Annie received the national 2004 Angel Soft Angels in Action Award and was named one of *Teen Magazine*'s "Top Teens Making a Difference." According to Annie, "The best reward I'll ever get is knowing I've made a difference in someone's life. Growing up, my parents always stressed to my brother and sister and me the importance of volunteering. If you choose to help out by doing something that you really enjoy and care about, then volunteering will be fun! I encourage you all to use your time, talents, and voices to make the world a better place."

Author's note: About ten years ago, a young man who needed the guidance of adult wisdom entered my life. After I helped him deal with some normal teenage angst, he told me his story of how his mother had abused him when he was six, his parents divorced, and he left his home with nothing but the clothes on his back. Perhaps with one of Annie's Care Bags, his transition would not have been quite so traumatic.

Dan Kent

Spotlight on: Dan Kent

Service Project Discussed: Computer education for senior citizens
Fundraiser Discussed: Matching gifts, direct donations

In May 2005, Dan Kent was identified as one of America's Top Ten Youth
Volunteers and received the Prudential Spirit of Community Award for
extraordinary community service. Dan began the journey to this honor several years earlier when he began teaching senior citizens how to use computers and access the Internet. He found that many seniors are disconnected
from their loved ones, so he set up classes at his school for them.

Then he realized that some senior citizens were unable to leave their
homes to attend his classes. He visualized setting up small computer labs at
senior citizen centers. When Dan contacted the administration at a few cen-

ters, he found that they were thrilled with the idea. Using his own savings, he purchased some computers and set up a Web site: www.seniorconnects.org. Over the next few months, he enlisted the help of student volunteers to collect donated computers, set up computer labs, and teach the classes.

Eventually, Dan found that he needed to establish his own 501(c)(3) nonprofit foundation. His purchases became tax-free and donations became deductible. It was a decision that would encourage individuals and corporations to donate enough money to keep Senior Connects operating in the ever-expanding network of independent living centers. He has received several matching grants and anonymous donations since he began his foundation. He and his staff of volunteers have raised over $120,000 in donations for the equipment and setup in over 70 senior centers.

Dan divided his young volunteers into two groups: those who refurbish computers and those who teach the classes. However, he eventually encountered a problem—very few of his volunteers drive, so they were unable to deliver the refurbished computers to the senior centers. Dan had originally partnered Senior Connects with Asset Forwarding, an Indianapolis electronics refurbishing company, to obtain the computers. The president of Asset Forwarding, Mark Vander, provided even more assistance by offering to deliver the computers directly to the senior citizen communities, where Dan and his team would set them up.

Senior Connects now has an active advisory board that looks for ways to improve their services to the seniors in the Indianapolis area. Volunteers with at least 12 months of service are eligible to serve on the board. The Senior Connects Foundation offers a yearly $100 prize for the best suggestion that enhances the program. They provide Certificates of Success based on three months of service and a recommendation from the senior care facility. For volunteers who have served at least six months, they will write a college or employment letter of recommendation that details the services the volunteers provided. They recognize the individual making the most significant contribution using the Senior Connects program with a VIP Award, which carries a $2,500 prize, plus six $500 prizes for runners-up.

Unlike high school classes of 20 students, the Senior Connects classes are very small, sometimes only one or two students. Also unlike high school classes, the young volunteers do not leave because the year is over or the forty-minute bell has rung. They stay until the seniors are comfortable with the knowledge they have presented that day. The following session, the volunteers build on the previous lesson. The majority of senior residents are interested in e-mailing their relatives and finding information about the weather or health issues on the Internet.

Dan and his team refuse payment from the people they serve. They prefer an e-mailed letter of appreciation sent to their Web site, indicating that the senior citizens have become proficient enough to do so. According to Dan, "Increasing senior citizen Internet literacy is extremely important to both seniors and their families. Empowering them to access the news and keep up to date with their passions and hobbies, research health questions, and keep in contact with family members through e-mail helps their world grow a little larger."

Jena Sims

Spotlight on: Jena Sims

Service Project Discussed: Fundraising for American Cancer Society
Fundraiser Discussed: Memorial ornaments, T-shirts

When Jena was eight and nine years old, she participated in the Georgia Relay for Life marathon, walking the track and playing games all night long with friends. She thought it was fun to raise money for a cure for cancer. Then when she was 10 years old, she lost both of her grandfathers to cancer and her efforts took on a new focus. She wanted to do more than walk and play games. That year, she became the youngest team captain for Relay for Life, organizing her own team of 10 members.

Jena wanted to do something original to help find the cure for the disease that took two family members from her life. While on a trip to Las Vegas, she saw ornaments for sale that had pieces of performers' clothing inside. She picked one up and an idea began to emerge. She would create and sell original ornaments for the American Cancer Society that would be in honor or in memory of someone.

For five months, she designed and created ornaments, trained a team of workers, marketed her idea, and built a Web site: www.ornaments4cure.org. With her team of 26 other teens, she made a video that aired on two channels, created T-shirts to advertise their campaign, spoke on radio programs, and copyrighted the ornament design. When they were ready, they began to sell the clear tinsel-filled ornaments.

They spoke at service organizations, such as Rotary and Lions' Clubs. Some of her team members were reluctant to speak before a group of adults, but with Jena's encouragement, each member stood up and spoke about the ornaments and the team's goals. Jena's team has sold over 1,500 ornaments at $10 each. With her other fundraisers such as cake walks, face-painting, yard sales, car washes, lock-ins, dances, and yard sign sales, they have earned over $64,000 for the American Cancer Society. Jena's goal is to raise $75,000 before she graduates from high school.

Next, she decided to bring her ornaments directly to the persons they benefited. With ornaments and supplies in a basket and administrative approval obtained, Jena went to the hospitals. There she helped the children and adults create and personalize their own ornaments. They picked out their own color ribbons and tinsel, and then wrote their name and the date on the ornament. She called this her "Joy of Giving" campaign. She gave away a thousand ornaments, but lost some of the profits in doing so. According to Jena, "Yes, I lost profits by giving away over one thousand ornaments, but it's OK. The priceless smiles on those kids' faces more than made up for lost money."

Jena has been recognized by the Georgia legislature for her efforts and was the recipient of a Prudential Spirit of Community Award. She has met celebrities and attended awards ceremonies. But these honors are not why Jena is so enthusiastic about her Ornaments4Cure. She says, "Today there are over nine million cancer survivors and this number is growing every day. So the money we are raising is certainly helping. You are never too young or old to volunteer and it can be so much fun!"

Trevor Barrott accepts the AXA Financial Scholarship from AXA Advisors Ryan Beck and Kelly Brown.

Spotlight on: Trevor Barrott

Service Project Discussed: Help for military families
Fundraiser Discussed: Christmas social, direct donations

In the spring of 2004, Trevor Barrott saw that friends of his family were called to active duty in Iraq. Until that moment it had never occurred to him that others make a sacrifice for his freedom. He also never realized the impact that their service had on their families, especially their children, both financially and emotionally.

Trevor took it upon himself to create an organization to offer support to the families of the 116th Cavalry of the Idaho Army National Guard. He first went to his school advisor to enlist her help and then went to meet with the Family Service Coordinator with the National Guard. Both enthusiastically agreed to help him.

His first plan of action was to get all school fees waived for military children in his school district. He met with his school superintendent, who agreed that the military families deserved special consideration. He then enlisted the help of five of his friends and formed a committee. They named their group "Dare to Care—Idaho Kids Caring for Idaho Military Families."

Trevor and his committee met with business executives as well as community organizations to help finance his program. With the help of the YFCA, Lamb Weston, Coca-Cola, Optimist Club, Lions Club, local media, state representatives and senators, and others, Dare to Care raised enough money to purchase school supplies and host a back-to-school party for military children.

When Trevor was asked to present his program at a state convention called "Speak Out for the Military Child," he was nervous at first, but received an overwhelming response when he had completed his presentation. Dare to Care was designed to help others, but while attending the state convention, Trevor found that he was the one who was helped the most. While spending time with military children, he says, "I gained a greater understanding and appreciation for the sacrifice that they make on behalf of my freedom."

Dare to Care has hosted many events for the military families since the inception of the program, including a mother-daughter summer luncheon, thank-you dinner baskets made by local church women and distributed to the military families, and a Halloween party for the children. In addition, Trevor and his friends collected hats, mittens, and coats for the children.

The program continues today. They have held a Christmas social, Valentine babysitting project to allow parents a night out, Easter egg hunt, and anything else they can do to help. The program has been adopted by Business

Professionals of America that will work to develop programs in their communities. It was also taken to a National Guard national convention where it was wholeheartedly received by other states. A letter was recently sent out to school superintendents around the state of Idaho encouraging them to waive school fees for military kids K through 12. This is now being accepted by many of those school districts. Also, there is a camp scheduled this summer for military families to be held in the South Hills of Twin Falls.

Although he will tell you that he is always surprised by the publicity he has received for his efforts, Trevor has received many prestigious awards. He won the Congressional Bronze, Silver, and Gold Medals, the Idaho Brightest Star Award, and was a recipient of the Prudential Spirit of Community State Award. He has also been awarded three scholarships: the Best Buy Scholarship, the Walton Scholarship, and the AXA Financial Scholarship.

Trevor's campaign began with one young person's desire to do something to show support and appreciation for the Idaho military. Channel One News, a news station broadcasted to high schools around the country, recognized his efforts by presenting a segment of programming on Dare to Care.

Today the Dare to Care initiative is expanding to other states. According to Trevor, after hosting a back-to-school party, "I am always amazed at how much the children of military personnel love to come and hang out with their peers and how grateful their families are to know that someone cares."

Author's note: I teach at a school district where one-third of our children come from military families. I see firsthand how the children react to having a parent go overseas. They don't know if they will ever see that parent again and it is emotionally stressing for them. Sometimes financial assets are not immediately available to the remaining spouse, so the children may not be able to get the supplies they need as soon as the teachers request them. Trevor's campaign provides solutions to a real need in the communities that serve the children of military families.

Augusta DeLisi

Spotlight on: Augusta DeLisi

Service Project Discussed: Save shelter dogs

Fundraiser Discussed: Pennies for Pound Puppies campaign, Chinese auction

When Augusta DeLisi was 12 years old, she explored an online dog adoption site, and what she saw appalled her. Eight dogs at a shelter in West Virginia were about to be euthanized in five days if they weren't adopted. Augusta called the shelter from her home in Pennsylvania so she could save the dogs. She persuaded her father to drive two and a half hours with her to the shelter to pick them up. On their way home, eight full-grown dogs clambered around and slobbered the windows of their Chevy Suburban.

Augusta placed them in local shelters, not a *Green Mile*-style shelter like the one in West Virginia where all the animals awaited euthanasia. The shelters where Augusta placed the dogs cared for them until they were adopted. Eventually, all eight were placed in good homes. By this time, Augusta was committed to saving as many dogs as she could.

Eventually, Augusta began bringing the dogs back to her home, which she shares with her parents, five brothers and sisters, and three dogs of their own. Everyone helps with the responsibilities of feeding, grooming, and cleaning up after the dogs. She now has three kennels in her basement. She added a padded floor and padded beds for their comfort.

When she brings a dog home from a shelter, she quickly sets the wheels in motion that will place the dog in an adoptive home.

When Augusta gets the dogs, they are not in optimum condition. Some have been starved; others have been beaten or neglected. All are in need of attention. So, she gives them a bath and a new collar, keeping the old collar in her "memory box." When the dogs are ready for a new family, she takes them for walks and to pet supply stores on adoption days. The dogs proudly wear orange and black "adopt me" vests. She hangs posters on bulletin boards and maintains a Web site that she designed (www.augiesdog-giesrescue.org), where she advertises the dogs ready for adoption. Look in the pet finder section of her Web site.

Augusta keeps up with the dogs' shots and medications. When the dog is old enough, she makes sure that it is spayed or neutered to prevent any other unwanted puppies. She cares for them as if they were her own, then releases them to their new families. At first she cried when they left, but now she smiles and takes their pictures with their new owners. Each picture goes into her ever-expanding memory box.

Augusta adopts all breeds of dogs. She usually chooses the dogs by their length of stay at the shelters. One miniature pinscher mix had been in a shelter for a year and a half when Augusta rescued him. He had been there so long that his only name was "Cage 55." She renamed him "Harley," and today he is enjoying a wonderful life with a new family.

Most of the expenses for her rescue efforts come from the family's own savings. The cost of taking in a dog is about $200. She charges people who adopt the dogs to offset some of her expenses, but she has found that she needs additional funds to cover the cost. So she organized "Pennies for Pound Puppies" at her school and held a "Party for Pound Puppies" at her house. Between the two, she raised $700. Eventually, she branched out to the community and sponsored a rescue event at a local recreation center, which included a Chinese auction and food in addition to several dogs begging for adoption. She actively seeks donations from individuals and companies on her Web site.

Augusta has rescued over eighty dogs and puppies from euthanasia. She says that the most rewarding feeling in the world is when one of the rescued dogs is adopted. When asked what others can do to help, she replied, "Volunteer and do whatever you can to help your local animal shelter. You can walk and socialize dogs, help them with fundraisers, or anything else they need. As long as you work hard, you can do anything you put your mind to."

Francesca Tenconi

Spotlight on: Francesca Tenconi

Service Project Discussed: Children's Skin Disease Foundation
Fundraiser Discussed: Sponsorships, direct donations

When Francesca Tenconi was 11 years old, she was diagnosed with pemphigus foliaceous, a potentially fatal genetic skin disease. She received many treatments at area hospitals and met dozens of children with similar skin diseases, all of whom needed treatment for their skin lesions. These diseases caused discomfort, pain, disfigurement, disability, dependency, or death, and they can also shatter children's self-esteem and cause financial and emotional burdens on their families. Over the years, Francesca knew that she needed to form a support group for her new friends. She wanted to begin a foundation to help them.

For Francesca's 16th birthday, she asked for nothing more than donations to help her form the Children's Skin Disease Foundation (CSDF). Four days after her birthday, on May 29, 2000, her dream became a reality. Francesca envisioned a network of researchers who worked to find cures for the skin diseases. She wanted a camp where the children could enjoy their vacation without shame or embarrassment. She wanted a support group for families of the children affected by skin diseases. She was a young lady with a mission.

One year after Francesca incorporated her 501(c)(3) foundation, CSDF began Camp Wonder at Camp Arroyo in Livermore, California. Supported by a grant from the Taylor Family Foundation, the camp offers a medical staff and recreational staff working together in a relaxed environment. At Camp Wonder, Francesca and her friends could swim, have campfires, do crafts, and play games while being treated by the doctors and nurses there.

Francesca is on the board of directors for her foundation, along with her parents and a family friend. Since the foundation began, the CSDF has helped some children obtain wheelchairs. They hold social and athletic events for the children and their families. They have set up a support group where families can go for information about skin diseases. They are working on a "Make-A-Wish" program for terminally ill children.

All of these goals need funds. Each camper attends free of charge because the families are usually burdened with many other expenses. They rely only on sponsorships, which come from corporate and private sponsors. Francesca asks for donations wherever she goes, both supplies for Camp Wonder and money for the research program. The foundation contacts medical professionals and asks them to volunteer to help dress the children's bandages, a time-consuming effort. The camps also need volunteer counselors to set up the activities.

Francesca's Web site, www.csdf.org, presents the wonderful work that her foundation continues to do since she began it several years ago. She has added two new camps in other parts of the country. Victory Junction Gang Camp is in Randleman, North Carolina, and Painted Turtle Camp is in Lake Hughes, California. She has also raised more than $100,000 to support research.

Francesca won the 2002 Prudential Spirit of Community Award for her efforts. The following year, she served on the selection committee that chose the 2003 winners. Eventually, Francesca's skin condition became controlled with medication. She enrolled at Duke University and soon thereafter, she received *Glamour* magazine's Top 10 College Women of 2005 award. She now runs her foundation from her dorm room. According to Francesca, "Beauty may be skin deep, but the physical and emotional harm caused by skin disease affects a child for life. All children with skin disease experience feelings of rejection like I did. They just want to be treated as normal children."

7

Real Projects with Real Instructions

"Every individual matters. Every individual has a role to play. Every individual makes a difference. And we have a choice: what sort of difference do we want to make?"

—Jane Goodall

Here are the directions for completing some of the projects and fundraisers discussed in previous chapters. Step-by-step instructions and valuable tips will help ensure the success of your projects and fundraisers. Some projects are for older children, while others are more appropriate for younger philanthropists. Choose the project that best suits the ages and interests of your group members.

Projects That Help Children

If your group of young philanthropists decides to help children, browse through this section. You'll find projects that require a bit of sewing, while others involve simple cutting and pasting. When children help children, everyone benefits from the effort.

Spotlight Project: Quilts for Kids

There are several organizations that distribute quilts to needy children. Annie Wignall includes quilts in some of her Care Bags (see pages 94–95). There are also national networks, such as Project Linus, that send quilts to social service organizations, hospitals, and police stations to help abused, abandoned, and other needy children.

Materials

2 yards or more of pre-washed fabric (this will make the smallest
    quilt for infants); 4 yards will make a quilt for a teenager
Quilt batting
Thread
Pins
Sewing machine
Embroidery floss (various colors)
Large hand needles
Optional: needle threader

Directions

1. Cut squares of fabric into six-inch squares. Children find it easier to
    use a cardboard template to trace onto the fabric, and then cut.
    When you have enough squares, machine sew them together in a pat-

tern or at random. Sew strips of squares from six to ten squares long, then sew six to ten strips next to each other to form the quilt top. Try to align the squares, but sometimes that is not possible. Remember that the goal is to provide warm, comfortable blankets for needy children, not works of art.

2. Pin the quilt top to the batting and cut so they are both the same size.

3. Place a solid piece of fabric under the top and batting, good side down. Cut so it is one inch larger than the top. (I use a yardstick laid along the length and draw a line along the outside edge.)

4. Turn the one-inch border up once, then twice, to enclose the raw edges. Sew close to the edge of the border.

5. With embroidery floss, sew knots in the center of each square. Go down from the top and come back up next to the first stitch. Tie together using a square knot. Trim to one-fourth inch. Check to see that the quilt is baby ready: all pins have been removed and all threads have been trimmed.

Feel free to add your own touches with fabric markers. Never use buttons or puffy paints.

If you are looking for other quilt patterns, go to www.freequiltpatterns.info or check out a quilting book at your local library. Send your quilts to the charity of your choice with a note indicating your group's name and address. Check the organization's Web site for additional information regarding signatures, and more. You could also place notices about your project in the local craft and fabric supply stores. You may be surprised how many quilts and blankets you receive as donations! Here are two Web sites with information on quilt collection: www.projectlinus.org and www.quiltsforcomfort.com.

Universal Picture Books

Children's hospitals sometimes look for unique books to leave in their waiting room. The most effective are those that are not bound by a specific language; that is, books that tell stories using pictures only. Contact your local hospitals and children's centers to find out their needs before beginning this project.

Materials

Pictures of animals, children, people, scenery, and more
9- by 12-inch poster board or construction paper
Ring binder for each picture book
Textured fabric
Glue
Laminator or self-stick plastic adhesive covering
3-hole punch

Directions

1. Create pages by pasting pictures onto poster board or construction paper. Have your members draw pictures that children would enjoy or take rubbings of common objects.
2. Assemble 10 to 15 pages, and then laminate them or cover with plastic adhesive covering.
3. Create a textured cover by gluing pieces of fabric onto a ring binder.
4. Punch holes in the pages and insert into the binder.

Bicycle Safety Fair

For the children in your own area, hold a bicycle safety fair that educates young children about bicycle safety. Here are some guidelines for a successful fair:

Directions

1. Enlist the aid of your local police department. Sometimes they have programs already in place that you can help to implement.
2. Arrange for a safe place to hold the fair, such as a school parking lot on a Sunday afternoon. This is a good choice, because there is usually little traffic from sports activities. Also see if you can use the gym or multipurpose room if it rains.
3. Advertise the date, time, and location of your fair. Make sure you require that children bring a helmet with their bicycle or tricycle.
4. Require preregistration so you can be prepared for the number of children who will participate. Consider limiting the number to 30 or 40 participants.
5. Divide your group in half to separate the preschool tricyclists from the elementary school bicyclists.

6. Show the proper way to put on a helmet before the children enter your course.

7. Have safety inspections of individual bicycles, testing the braking system, horn, reflectors, chains, and lights.

8. Set up a course using traffic cones.

9. Develop a list of scenarios that the children need to understand: traffic lights, intersections, one-way roads, horns, and more. Let the children ride the course as your members stand at stations "testing" their ability to cope with situations.

10. Show a video on bicycle safety while they have refreshments after they "graduate." Determine whether you want to charge for refreshments or not, depending on your financial situation.

11. Prepare certificates of participation to help them remember what they learned.

12. Have a donations can available for parents who want to help support your projects.

13. Make sure you have a poster that describes your group and its goals.

Projects for Senior Citizens

Sometimes children need a nudge to consider doing projects for senior citizens. The projects suggested in this section might be more acceptable to your group after a visit to the local nursing home. These projects all help the senior citizens feel accepted as part of the larger community.

Personal Wreaths

When senior citizens become residents at a care facility, they sometimes find that their identity becomes blurred with the other residents. They are no longer in the home that they lived in for many years. They may not have daily contact with friends and family. More than likely, they brought with them only a few personal possessions. This project helps to restore some of their individuality while building a bond between the older and younger people.

Prepare your young people to meet with the senior citizens by discussing how they are just like us, but older. Explain how everyone needs to be treated with dignity and respect. You might want to go to the nursing home ahead of time to take pictures of the meeting area and some of the residents. Find out how many residents would be interested in participating in the project. This will let you know whether the contact will be one on one, whether you will have two young people with one older person, or vice versa. When the children know what to expect, they will be less fearful of the nursing home experience.

Directions

1. Arrange with the administration of the nursing home to visit on a regular schedule. You will need to meet with each senior two times to complete this project.
2. The objective of the first meeting is to get to know each other so your young members will know what to include on the personal wreaths.
3. Prepare a list of questions that can jump-start the conversation. Sometimes the children are too shy to talk to the residents. Always ask permission to take the senior citizen's photograph, and then ask open-ended questions such as:

- Describe where you were born.
- Tell me a story about your childhood.
- Talk about your first job.

- What did you do on Sunday afternoons with your family?
- Tell me about your children.
- What did you like to do when the chores were done?
- What is your favorite color, sport, and animal?

4. Around two weeks after the first contact, the children will bring a wreath base, tacky glue, and decorations. The wreath could be straw, stained or painted wood, quilted fabric, or artificial greens. They should create a sign with the resident's name on it and have the photograph ready that may have been taken. The children should also have things that are reminiscent of the conversation. For example, if a

man says that he played baseball when he was younger, his young partner could put a picture of a baseball and bat on his wreath. If a woman likes to knit, her young partner could have a bit of twisted yarn on her wreath. It's important to have enough of a conversation with the nursing home resident so the young person can have several individualized items on the wreath. Finally, they should have decorative items such as bows, flowers, ribbons, and plastic fruit.

5. During the personal wreath workshop, the children will ask the residents where they would like to place the items that they have brought with them. When they are done, they can share the wreath with other residents in a roundtable discussion and then hang it on the door or over the bed of the senior.

Author's note: This initial contact should not be the end of the story. Most seniors look forward to their young guests. Use any of the other suggestions presented here for further visits.

Talent Show

For this project, you need to make sure that participating students have some form of talent. If you have a few who can sing, play instruments, or do stand-up comedy, then proceed with this plan. This project would probably be the very last one for the year, as it takes a long time to plan and rehearse. Remember, you don't need to limit your presentation to the nursing home that you have adopted. Reach out to other senior citizen homes and communities. Here are some guidelines for a successful talent show:

• Arrange this event with the administration well in advance of your anticipated performance date. Talk about the location, time, date, and refreshments.

- Begin with a time line that includes planning time, printing of programs, and rehearsals.
- Balance your talent show with music, magic, speaking, comedy, and
  group efforts such as skits.
- Encourage the children to develop acts that are age-appropriate for the
  seniors. In other words, encourage them to research what were the
  popular music, movies, and entertainers at the time when these seniors
  were young adults or possibly newlyweds.
- Print programs so the residents can follow along and know the names
  of the young talent performing for them.
- Include costumed performers for added interest.
- Add props such as stuffed animals, a cane, a top hat, and so forth.
- Have at least four rehearsals, including one dress rehearsal.
- As with old-fashioned vaudeville performances, you can have a person
  who holds up a sign that reads "Applause." This will be a great source
  of encouragement to the young person who feels self-conscious about
  performing.
- Always, always include a sing-along with printed words in the program. These are very popular.
- Bring snacks and beverages or arrange with the staff for refreshments
  so the senior citizens and young people can mingle after the
  performance.

Personal Journal

Many senior citizens have wonderful stories to tell, but have few people who
are willing to listen. Your young members can record their older friends'
memories in a journal that can be added to each time they get together.
Encourage the children to add their own touches to the journal—drawings,
diagrams, or cut-out pictures. Encourage the children to write neatly and
in complete sentences to develop their journaling skills.

Letter Writing

Some senior citizens have problems with eyesight and hand coordination that prevent them from being able to write letters to their relatives. Have your children buy or make attractive stationery and bring stamps. Alert the staff that you will need addresses of the residents' families. On the day of your visit, the children will then write the letters, have the senior citizen sign it himself, and the child can even add her own note at the bottom that she transcribed the letter. On the opposite end of this project, some senior citizens may receive mail from family members, but are unable to read the letters. Your youth group members can then read the letters and answer them during the same visit.

Cooking for One or Two

This project is suitable for the math teacher who is searching for an educational philanthropic project. Using recipes gathered from cookbooks or family recipe collections, the children can scale down the recipes to one or two servings. Each child would submit two or three typed recipes. Print as many copies of the recipes as you need for the senior citizen community that you have chosen. Create covers that have a catchy title and the name of your school or group. Laminate for durability. Bind them with plastic binding combs. If your school district does not have a binding machine available, go to your local office supply store. To offset the cost of printing, laminating, and binding, sell ads to be placed on the back cover. The usual customers might be food suppliers and flower shops. Also, contact the parents of children in your class to see if they would buy ad space.

Projects to Help the Environment

Many young people care about preserving the environment because they know that it will be theirs for the next 80 years. In this section, you will find projects that a young environmentalist can do on his own or with a group. Some projects work better in a rural environment, while others lend themselves to the urban environment.

Temporary Bird Houses

When permanent birdhouses are set up in a neighborhood, it is necessary to clean the bottom of the birdhouse each year to protect against the buildup of harmful bacteria from droppings. This project will enable your young environmentalists to provide safe homes for the birds. At the end of the summer, they should discard the birdhouses.

Materials

Empty half-gallon milk container or nondairy creamer container
Brown or green paint
Scissors
3-inch long dowel (I find that golf pencils work rather well!)
Moss
String
Stapler
Hole punch
Flat exterior varnish

Directions

1. Open the top of the container, and wash it, rinse it, and let it dry.
2. Cut a 2- to 3-inch hole 4 inches down from the top of the container.
3. Pierce a hole in the container ½-inch below the hole and insert the dowel. Glue into place.
4. If you use a milk carton, staple the top of it back together again.

5. Paint the container. When it dries, paint with the varnish, then glue on moss, grass, or leaves in various places.
6. Punch a hole in the top of the milk carton and insert a string for hanging; tie a string around the neck of the nondairy creamer container.
7. Hang near a source of water and food (berries, seed feeder, and so forth).

Campaign for the Environment

Your group could certainly participate in the Adopt-a-Road program and pick up trash along the road. However, to truly bring environmental awareness into the community, it is important to launch a campaign. Investigate the needs of your community and meet them with your campaign. Perhaps the schools do not recycle, or there are fast-food wrappers strewn along the roadways. The campaign has three segments: fliers, presentations, and requests for help. A successful campaign identifies one or two critical environmental concerns and alerts the community on how the residents can help.

- *Fliers*: Create colorful, yet simply presented, fliers. They should identify the problem and suggest a solution. Then they should be placed where residents can easily pick one up. For example, if your area's problem involves wrappers from fast-food restaurants, ask the management if you can place your fliers near the cash registers.
- *Presentations*: This segment requires that the young people develop a skit that could be presented at school or town meetings. Here are guidelines for presenting a successful skit:

  1. Limit the skit to no more than 10 minutes.
  2. Allow children to improvise, rather than memorize lines. This makes the skit more spontaneous and can often create a humorous situation. Prompt from off-stage if necessary.
  3. Practice speaking loudly, clearly, and slowly. Most children speak softly and quickly when they perform before a group. This is a great confidence-booster, as well.
  4. Have some props, but not so many that they become unmanageable or get in the way.
  5. Scenery is unnecessary with skits. If you feel it is necessary to place your audience in time or space, a narrator can do that nicely by reading a description.
  6. If the young actors speak to each other, have them turn so they partially face the audience. A soliloquy where one actor talks about the importance of your environmental project should be less than a minute long and be directed toward the audience.
  7. Include humor to break up the seriousness of your message. Consider this scenario:

Joe: Just how bad is the pollution at Lake Madison?

Amelia: It's so bad that the storks are bringing little oxygen tanks instead of baby fish.

8. Young people who absolutely refuse to speak during the skit can walk across the stage carrying a message on a stick. Sometimes this simple action can cause the audience to roar with laughter, depending on the message and its placement in the skit.

9. End with a punch. All of your members could return to the stage and shout your slogan or message. Or a talented member could write an original song that is accompanied by familiar music and distribute the words to the audience for a sing-along. However you decide to end your skit, the audience should immediately know that it has ended.

- *Requests for Help*: If your group is cleaning up a section of Landing Road, for example, you could distribute fliers to each residence asking for help on the days that your group will be picking up trash. Remember that U.S. Postal Service regulations prohibit the placing of anything but U.S. mail in or on the mailboxes. Therefore, you might hand deliver your fliers or use some other means of distribution, such as placing them in the local convenience store.

    You could go to a town meeting and present your concerns about the pollution that is occurring at a local lake. However, it is even better to go armed with suggestions for the cleanup process. Outline how your group will start the effort and how the town's residents can help. Reporters generally attend town meetings, so you may get free publicity for your project by taking this approach.

    Finally, wherever you advertise your campaign, you can certainly ask for financial support to help pay for trash collection bags, recycling bins, and stationery for your fliers.

Urban Garden

Empty urban lots tend to collect more than their fair share of trash. Before your group begins to plant an urban garden, they need to get permission from the city to clean it up and plant an attractive garden. Most cities are more than happy to oblige a group of young people who want to beautify the environment. You could even investigate the possibility of having the lot completely fenced in with a locked gate to prevent destruction of your efforts.

Once permission is obtained, you can begin the cleanup process. Safety is the biggest concern here. There may be sharp, dangerous objects, items that have contained hazardous fluids, or rash-producing plants. Make sure your young members wear long pants, heavy work gloves, and hard-soled shoes. Remind your little environmentalists to always look where they put their hands before picking something up in order to reduce injury from sharp objects. Better yet, tell them to only use tools to remove the trash. Rakes, shovels, and pliers safely remove both large and small pieces of trash. Empty the trash into a dumpster or cans that you will immediately transport to the dump. This is a time-consuming process for young people who like to see immediate results. When they are done, provide sanitizing hand lotion or access to soap and water. Make the day fun by providing food, drinks, and music.

If your lot backs up to a building, get additional permission to paint a mural on the side of the building. Perspective is important for this picture. Have a talented member draw in the outline for a long, country path or an Italian villa, perhaps. Other members can paint inside the lines. Always do the mural before planting the garden to avoid trampling.

With the lot cleaned and the mural painted, you can begin the process of planting the Urban Garden. Consider planting vegetables for distribution to the local soup kitchen. You might plant a flower garden for cutting, and then distribute the flowers to the charitable organization of your choice. Or you could plant a perennial butterfly garden.

As with any garden, the Urban Garden needs constant attention, including watering, weeding, and pruning. Assign a schedule where your members and their parents can tend the garden. Bring in a professional agriculturalist from your county extension office to help the members understand the proper way to tend their garden. Your group could turn an eyesore into eye candy for the residents who live around your Urban Garden.

Projects for Active and Retired Military Personnel

Whether you live near a military base or not, many children feel strongly that our troops, both active and veteran, need our support. Some of these projects are specifically for veterans who live in your community. Other projects help to make life a little easier for the men and women serving our country overseas.

Braille Flag

When veterans become blinded during active duty or because of medical complications, they are no longer able to see, the American flag that they served under so proudly. This Braille flag project brings the flag back to them in a way that allows them to feel, rather than see, the American flag. Contact your local veterans' hospitals and nursing homes to see how many veterans would be interested in your flags.

Materials

50 crystal tri-beads (11 mm)
9- by 12-inch sheet of white foam board
9- by 12-inch sheet of blue felt

9- by 12-inch sheet of red satin (or another smooth cloth)

White or blue thread

Needle

Glue

Directions

1. Cut the blue felt into a 4½- by 6-inch rectangle. Arrange the crystal tri-beads on the felt and lightly glue in place. Sew each one on individually by coming up through the hole, then going down on the outside of the bead. Go from bead to bead and row to row, sewing each bead onto the blue felt. (I tried using only glue and I found that the action of veterans' fingers on the stars causes them to pull off. Sewing them holds them in place very well.) Provide a flag for your junior philanthropists to view while placing the stars. Veterans with little to do will naturally finger the placement of the stars and may

count them over and over. You may want to check the placement for accuracy before your children sew the stars in place.

2. Cut the white foam down to 8 by 12 inches. Glue the blue felt into place.

3. Cut seven red stripes out of the satin: four ⅝ inches by 6 inches and three ⅝ inches by 12 inches.

Refer to the picture on page 128 to position each of these properly on the white backing, then glue into place.

Veterans Day Recognition Ceremony

If your town does not already have a Veterans Day ceremony, you can begin a tradition that could continue for many years after your youth group has gone on to college.

Schedule your ceremony as close to November 11 as possible, then follow these steps for a fun day for the veterans and the youth group participants.

- Since the weather will probably not cooperate to allow an outdoor ceremony unless you live in a warm climate, reserve a meeting room at your local library or community center.
- Invite veterans to your event by publicizing it in the newspaper at least a month ahead of time. Also send fliers to veterans' organizations listed in your local telephone directory. Be sure to look under Department of Veterans Affairs in the Federal Government listings. List the day, time, and events for the day, and encourage attendance with family and friends. Add your name or a mature member's name and phone number as a contact person. On the flier, ask the veterans to wear their medals.

- Provide incentives for participating. Have refreshments, a guest speaker, entertainment, or prizes. Refreshments should be simple: sweets, finger foods, and beverages. The guest speaker could be an active-duty military person speaking about his experiences overseas. Your members could create a skit about how they appreciate the work done by veterans in previous wars. Prizes could be for the oldest attendee, the one with the most years of military service, or the veteran with the most children or grandchildren.

- Your program should be no more than one hour, with another hour for refreshments and conversation. Begin with the posting of colors and Pledge of Allegiance. The Daughters of the American Revolution post the Pledge of Allegiance and flag protocol at this location on their Web site: http://dar.org/natsociety/Citizenship.cfm?TP=Show&ID=63#code. If you have a talented member, you could have her sing or play the National Anthem. Include a moment of silence for the military personnel who gave their lives.

- Sponsor an essay contest at the elementary schools: Why our town's veterans deserve our thanks. Choose the winner using a panel composed of a teacher, a veteran, and a member of your group. Have the winner read his or her essay at the ceremony, then give the winner a prize. Savings bonds are the usual prize, but you might also decide to offer a gift certificate that the young person can use immediately. You'll need to plan this ahead of time so the details can be included in your press materials, and provide a deadline before the event so judges will have time to select a winner.

- Introduce your guest speaker, who should have a mix of humor and serious content to the speech. Try to get someone to volunteer for this.

- To decorate the room, sponsor a poster contest with the same theme as the essay contest. Also announce this contest ahead of time as indicated above for the essay contest. Choose a winner and award ribbons and prizes. Other decorations might include red, white, and blue banners and flags.

- Have awards presentations for the veterans. Give a gift, perhaps a book or plant, to the veteran with the longest service, the oldest veteran, youngest veteran, etc. Give all attendees flag pins attached to handwritten or printed thank-you notes.
- Near the end of your ceremony, have fun with your members' skit or a game using some of the veterans as contestants. You can create a Power Point program, poster, or overhead of a Jeopardy show. Have the young people research questions that relate to military history.
- Conclude the formal ceremony with a retiring of colors while patriotic music plays.
- During refreshments, play more patriotic music and marches.
- Finally, remember to place a donation can at a table near the door so the attendees can support your philanthropic project and so you'll have seed money for the program for next year. Place copies of your newsletter or informational fliers there, too. Have a member sit at that table to answer questions.

Cooling Neckerchiefs

Polymer granules, when inserted into a cotton scarf, will absorb moisture, expand, and cool the wearer for many hours. If your group has access to sewing machines, you can easily make these neckerchiefs for the military serving in hot countries. Due to restrictions for military personnel receiving unsolicited mail, I recommend that you distribute your neckerchiefs to local family members of military personnel. They can then include your gift with theirs when they send their next care package to a loved one. The directions on the next page will make 55 neckerchiefs.

Materials

11 yards of lightweight 100% cotton fabric in camouflage design

1 pound water-absorbing polymer granules*

Dark green thread

Needle

Pins

Scissors or rotary cutter

Iron

Point turner

Gift tags

String for tying gift tag to neckerchief

*Available online. Comparison shop for the best price; some offer free samples that will fill one neckerchief. Go to www.watersorb.com and www.watercrystals.com.

Directions

1. Cut strips of fabric 7 inches by 45 inches. (You should be able to get 5 strips from each yard of fabric. I find that folding the fabric evenly and using a rotary cutter is easier and more accurate than using scissors.)

2. Fold fabric strip in half lengthwise, right sides together. Cut a triangular piece from each end to form points when you are done.

3. Pin neckerchief along cut edges. Mark off a 1½-inch section at center of tie. Do not sew in that area. That will be where you fill with the polymer granules.

4. Sew a ⅜-inch seam, leaving the center marked section open. Trim edges and turn. Push the points out with a point turner. Press the tie flat.

5. Measure 10 inches from each pointed end and sew across the tie from seam to fold (a horizontal row of stitches). This creates the pocket for

A gift to you from the
North Hamilton 4-H Sewing Club

Thank you for serving our country.
We appreciate all that you do for us.

To use your cooling neckerchief, soak it in water for 45 minutes
and the granules will expand. Remove and pat gently with a towel
to remove excess water. The neckerchief will help you stay cool
for hours. For extra cooling, soak and freeze the neckerchief.

your granules. Make sure you backstitch at both beginning and end
of the stitching line to secure this section.

6. Insert only 2 teaspoons of the polymer granules into the opening.
   Note: Although the polymers are nontoxic by EPA standards, it is a
   good idea to wear a dust mask while filling the neckerchiefs. Sew the
   opening shut. Attach gift tag. See above for sample text to include. Be
   sure to include instructions on how to use the neckerchief.

Projects for the Hospitalized

If you help your young people understand how important emotional health is to physical health, they will eagerly embrace projects for those who are hospitalized. Bring in a health care professional to speak with your group so they can hear firsthand how important the projects will be to the people in the hospital.

Crisis Bags

When adults are hospitalized, it helps to know that strangers care and want to help. These Crisis Bags are easy to create and offer comfort to those who might become despondent about their situation.

Your young philanthropists can collect or make bags of any kind—plastic, paper, hand sewn, or purchased. Then, during a meeting, you can fill them with comforting items, such as:

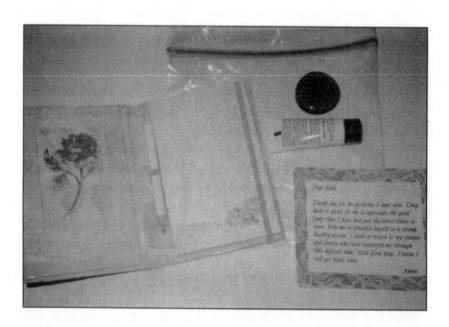

- Non-denominational prayers
- Words of wisdom or poems from a professional source
- Worry stone (Find a smooth, flat stone three or four inches wide and about a half inch high. Enclose a note with the stone that says, "A worry stone will ease your heart. Rub it so your worries depart.")
- New, small stuffed animal
- Pretty postcard, picture, or photograph
- Pocket packs of tissues (hospital tissues can be less soft than commercial tissues)
- A small bouquet of silk flowers
- A note that says, "I care about you," with the young person's signature (first name only)

Hospital Cart à la Carte

In most hospitals, volunteers travel room to room pushing a cart of supplies that help to make the patient's stay more pleasant. The items on that cart are generally supported by donations. To help with this effort, contact your local hospital to find out what is most needed. However, here is a list of some items that your group can collect:

- Books (new and gently used) for all ages
- Magazines (new and gently used) for all interests
- Pencils and pens
- Puzzles and puzzle books
- Small crafts in plastic bags (complete with small containers of glue, blunt-point needles, yarn, plastic canvas, counted cross-stitch patterns, and so forth)
- Stationery with envelopes or postcards

- Art supplies (paper, colored pencils, markers, and so forth) in kit form
- Stickers
- Jewelry
- New, small stuffed animals
- Hair clips
- Playing cards
- Games
- Toys for younger patients

Projects to Help Preserve History

Historic preservation projects help young people understand the history of their community. To encourage participation in these projects, invite a local historian to talk about the events that shaped their town. This person may also suggest projects in addition to the ones provided in this section.

Graveyard Records Preservation

Graveyards provide a snapshot history of the lives of those who lived in your town long before your members were born. The gravestone inscriptions may include information about the person's life in addition to date of death. With this project, children gain an appreciation of the rich culture that created their town while they preserve a gold mine of otherwise lost and forgotten information. Before beginning a graveyard records project, make sure that the local historical or genealogical society has not already done a similar project. If not, contact them anyway to let them know about your plans. Your young people may be able to work with the members of these other organizations to achieve a common goal. If you need to start from scratch, here is how you would go about recording the information in a permanent format:

- Take pictures. A digital camera will allow you to see the quality of your photographs before leaving the cemetery. Take two pictures of each gravestone—one up close so you can read the inscription and the other from a distance so you can identify the general location of the gravestone. Take pictures early on a clear day to get the most contrast on the etched tombstones. To enhance inscriptions that may have been worn away by time, spray the tombstone with water and let it dry for a few minutes. The face will dry first, leaving the inscription dark due to the moisture. You can also create shadows by using a mirror to reflect sunlight onto the tombstone until you achieve the desired effect. Note that the photographic method of preservation is generally preferable to taking rubbings, which can damage delicate headstone inscriptions.

- Go to the library. After making a list of the names found in the graveyard, search the library for tidbits of information about those former residents. Look in old newspapers that will probably be on microfilm. Check the Internet for death records, which may give information about living relatives of the deceased. Check the census records to see if you can find the homes that these people lived in. Enlist the aid of reference librarians, who are usually very happy to help with local research projects. They may know of obscure resources that will be very helpful to your research.

- Create the scrapbook. Organize your historical preservation book in some way—chronologically, alphabetically, or geographically. On each page, place the printed pictures of the gravestone, then add other information you have gathered. You might have the copy of a census record, a picture of the home the person lived in, and you may even be fortunate enough to find an old photograph of that person in the newspaper. For interest, add clip art and borders to your scrapbook.

- Publish your findings. When all the pages are assembled, duplicate them and bind them. The easiest way to do this is to take the pages to the local office supply store to make collated copies and bind with a plastic spiral. You might even get the store to donate materials for your project.
- Advertise your booklet. With one hundred copies of your booklet, charging $10 per copy and using donated materials, you could earn a thousand dollars for your group. This achieves a number of goals: Your group does a charitable project, they help preserve the history of your town, they form a bond by working together, and they have a fundraising effort that doubles as philanthropy.

Oral History Records

In each community, there are usually several senior members who recall a simpler lifestyle in that town. Contact the local historical society for the names of these individuals. Call and ask to interview them. Record their stories about schools, churches, transportation, weather, life at home, and any other topic they care to discuss. Type their account and then show it to them for approval. Take their pictures and add them to their memories. Reproduce, bind, and distribute the booklets you have created. This can either be a simple community service project or you can charge a small fee for the booklets as a fundraiser.

Miscellaneous Projects

There are certainly many, many other projects that your young philanthropists might want to pursue. Here are a few suggestions that will help people in your community.

Cholesterol Reduction Campaign

This is a good project for nutrition students. After investigating the difference between good and bad cholesterol, have the students make lists of cholesterol-friendly foods and distribute that list to patrons as they enter the local grocery store. (Remember to get permission from the manager first!)

Book Collections

Practically everyone has books on their shelves that they have read and no longer want. Your members can post a collection time and place to gather these books and distribute them to women's shelters, veterans' hospitals, nursing homes, and any other local organizations that may need books for their residents, patients, or the community they serve.

Station WWCD (What We Can Do)

If your school has its own television or radio station, your members can create a weekly or monthly broadcast about ways that other students can help in the community. Spotlight a specific project—animal shelter, road cleanup campaign, and so forth—during each program. You can also set up your own Web site or broadcast from the school public address system for the same purpose.

Bags for the Homeless

Just as Annie Wignall provides her Care Bags for needy children, your group can provide tote bags for the homeless. Fill the bags with toiletries, warm gloves and hats, gift certificates for food, and any other items you think a homeless person might appreciate.

Online Projects That Your Group Can Support

If you have access to the Internet and would like to do a philanthropic effort without even leaving home, consider the projects in this section. Sometimes with a simple daily click, your group can support a worthy cause. Some of these Web sites require a purchase to support the charity.

www.booksforsoldiers.com

After completing a notorized application to prevent unauthorized shipments to our military personnel, you can ship books, magazines, and other welcomed items to the troops stationed overseas.

www.heifer.org

Heifer International provides animals to people in less developed areas of the world to help them become self-sufficient. By giving them animals, rather than food, and the education to care for the animals, Heifer International helps people earn a living while feeding their families.

www.charityUSA.com

Although this is a commercial site, it has links to Web sites that provide donations to charitable organizations for each of the products ordered through them. With every item you buy, you generate funding that makes a difference for a variety of worthy causes. You might also use these sites in conjunction with your other philanthropic work. For example, at one of their sister sites, www.therainforestsite.com, your little environmentalists can buy holiday gifts for their family while supporting rain forest preservation.

www.thenonprofits.com

Without spending a penny, you can donate to your favorite charities by visiting their Web sites. Commercial sponsors provide the backing for this effort. Link to their Web site every day to encourage the sponsors to donate more money.

You'll find Web sites that suggest additional charitable projects in the Resources section in the back of this book.

Part III

Additional Information

"With support for volunteering and service at its highest level ever, together we can seize the momentum and build a culture of service and a nation of volunteers."

—David Eisner, CEO of the Corporation
for National and Community Service

Evaluation Information

In their *How-to Guide for Reflection*, the National Service Learning Cooperative says, "All thinking and dialogue requires some form of reflection if learning is to take place." This is so true with philanthropy. When your children plan and carry out their charitable projects and fundraisers, it is important to reflect on the effectiveness of these endeavors.

Reflection and evaluation help children better understand themselves and their abilities. They help children see the many ways their project has touched people, and not just their immediate target group. For example, when a youth group helps out at a nursing home, not only are the residents helped because they feel better (more fulfilled), but you also help ease the workload of the overtaxed staff, and you help other family members of residents feel that the senior members of their family are being cared for in a special way.

Evaluations are also important if you are using grant funds for your project. Most foundations require justification of their disbursed funds. When used with your financial sheets, the evaluation documents should satisfy this requirement. Use any or all of the evaluation methods presented here to enhance the learning of your young people, to see how well you are proceeding as a leader, and to provide justification documents.

Journals

Many children shy away from journals because they are required in English class. When an activity is required, some children may equate it with an undesirable activity. However, journals are one of the best ways to record service learning activities while adding an element of emotional appeal. To offset this negative perception of journals, you could tell your members that their journals will become the basis for discussion during an end-of-the-year retreat. Help them to record their service in a small notebook. The only information needed would be the date, time, activity, and a simple comment. Some ambitious writers will fill their entire notebook; others will only fill a few pages. You might also encourage the children to include photographs in their journals. At the end of the year, they will be amazed at how much they accomplished, how much they learned, and how much they helped. The journal can also become a valuable memory-box item to later remind your members of the good work they did when they were younger.

Formal Evaluation

I think most youth group leaders, teachers, and parents use some form of evaluation device to help them understand how well their project went. Teachers have final exams, youth group leaders pass out evaluation forms, and parents may have dinner-table discussions. They use the evaluation as a basis for discussion with the service learning journals to create a complete package for their members. I find that open-ended questions provide the most comprehensive feedback, whereas a simple numbered evaluation provides superficial thought. You can decide whether you want the forms to remain anonymous.

You can also decide whether you want to allow the children to take the form home and return it at the next meeting, which may not happen, or whether you want to devote an entire meeting session to completing the evaluation. If you devote an entire meeting session at the end of the year to evaluation, create a comfortable environment by providing snacks and playing soft music while they think and write to discourage discussion until everyone is done. Some will finish earlier than others, so plan a quiet activity for them in another room or a separate area of your meeting room until everyone completes this process. During discussion time, either collect and read the forms to protect members' anonymity, or ask individuals to share their answers with the group.

Here is a sample evaluation form, which you can adjust to suit your individual needs. You can insert specific projects and activities instead of the general references that I have provided to personalize these questions. You might distribute the evaluation form after each project or at the end of the year. You'll get better answers if you ask specific questions. These questions work well for teens; you may need to adjust the questions for younger members.

Philanthropy Evaluation

A. Preparation
   1. When we had activities to choose a charitable project, which one did you enjoy most and why?
   2. How could we have improved the planning process for our projects?
   3. What was your favorite part of the preparation process?
   4. Did you feel you were a valuable part of the planning? Explain.
B. Project
   1. What was your favorite part of the project and why?
   2. What surprised you about our project?
   3. Comment on the overall time we spent doing the project—too much, too little, or just right?
   4. How could the project be improved?

C. Evaluation
   1. If this was your first time volunteering, how have you changed?
   2. If this was not your first time volunteering, how was this experience different from other volunteer efforts?
   3. What did you learn from doing the project?
   4. How could you have improved your participation during the project?
   5. How might we encourage other people to join our volunteer efforts?

Teacher/Leader Evaluation

Paper recording systems just don't work for me anymore. I love the convenience and efficiency of storing data on the computer. Therefore, I will share with you how to set up an evaluation database for your students. Unless you are knowledgeable about formal databases, such as Microsoft Access, and can set up many variables easily, you can simply do what I do: use a simple spreadsheet program such as Microsoft Excel or similar software.

Begin with Sheet 1 and create a listing of your members' vital information. Include first and last names, addresses, phone numbers, e-mail addresses, parents' names, parents' e-mail addresses, and other information. That last column can contain allergy information, medication information, and any other information the parent or child shares with you about special conditions or needs.

On Sheet 2, you will record attendance. List the dates of your meetings and projects across the top and names of your members down the left column. Enter O for on time, L for late, and X for absent. When a new member joins, you only need to highlight the student names and data, then re-sort in alphabetical order.

On Sheet 3, you can record individual information. Across the top, list characteristics such as dependability, initiative, flexibility, enthusiasm, independence, follows directions, communication, group player, leader, and any other characteristics you find valuable. Record comments regularly, perhaps four times each year, about each member. By recording the date of the comment, you can see how the young people grow throughout the year. You can do this easily by formatting all cells to wrap text. This keeps your data in one cell for each member and criterion.

The Formal Evaluation

Your students have completed their forms and you have kept track of their progress. Perhaps you have led a group discussion of the year's programs and projects. Is that the end of the story? Not according to Project STAR (Support and Training for Assessing Results). You need to keep an assessment log for each project to adequately predict success the following year. Here are some of their tips for accurately assessing your charitable project:

- List goals early in the planning process. During evaluation, respond to each objective, noting degree of success.
- Results should not describe the process. Instead of saying that you spent $100 and 300 hours, describe who or what you helped and how.
- List measurable outcomes. This is especially important if you are using grant money. Did you save 20 dogs from euthanasia? Did you serve meals to 50 senior citizens? Be specific with your evaluation.
- Use previous years' outcomes as baseline data. If you served 25 meals to the Ronald McDonald House residents last year, tell how many you served during this evaluation year. Compare results.

- Include qualitative as well as quantitative data. Did you improve the quality of life for hospital residents? How do you know that? Your answers may come from oral or written surveys.
- Identify a standard for each measure listed. If your goal is to write letters to the military overseas, then tell how many you expect to write. During evaluation, it will be easier to see if you met your goal.

The Bottom Line: An evaluation is as important to the success of future projects as the planning is to current projects.

Resources

The books, videos, and Web sites listed here provide teachers, parents, and youth group leaders with discussion starters and background information. Perhaps your children already have an idea of what they want to do as their philanthropic project. If so, then you can read a story or show a video on that topic. If your children are undecided, then choose one of the general interest books and videos. The resources have the suggested age designations: P (Preschool), E (Elementary), M (Middle School), and T (Teen).

Books to Jump-Start Your Program

Books About Basic Helpfulness

The Berenstain Bears Think of Those in Need by Jan and Stan Berenstain. New York: Random House Books for Young People, 1999. (The Berenstain family of bears donates their extra stuff to charity.) P

A Chair for My Mother by Vera Williams. New York: Greenwillow, 1982. (Collecting a few coins frequently adds up to a lot of coins that make a difference.) P

Changes, Changes by Pat Hutchins. New York: Alladin, 1987. (This book without words encourages children to make up their own stories of how people overcome hardship through adversity.) P

The Children's Book of Heroes by William J. Bennett. New York: Simon and Schuster, 1997. (Pick appropriate stories from this collection of mini-biographies.) E

The Giving Book: Open the Door to a Lifetime of Giving by Ellen Sabin. New York: Watering Can Press, 2004. (Use as a scrapbook, workbook, and motivational book.) E

How Kind! by Mary Elizabeth Murphy. Cambridge, MA: Candlewick Press, 2004. (One good deed deserves another.) P

Kids' Random Acts of Kindness by Conari Press, editors. Berkeley, CA: Conari Press, 1994. (Motivational stories for younger kids.) P/E

Leah's Pony by Elizabeth Friedrich. Honesdale, PA: Boyds Mills Press, 1996. (Set during the Great Depression, this book will help children understand the value of true sacrifice.) P

The Legend of the Bluebonnet by Tomie dePaola. New York: Putnam Juvenile, 1996. (A Native American child sacrifices her only possession to end a famine.) P

Let's Talk About Being Helpful by Joy Berry. New York: Scholastic, 1996. (It is important to begin with helpfulness at home.) P

Miss Rumphius by Barbara Cooney. New York: Puffin, 1985. (We all need to do one thing to make the world more beautiful before we die.) P

The Mitten Tree by Candace Christiansen. New York: Scholastic, 1997. (Although this book has an old woman as the main character, it teaches children about compassion for others.) P

More Random Acts of Kindness by Conari Press, editors. Berkeley, CA: Conari Press, 1994. (More stories to inspire action.) E/M/T

Now One Foot, Now the Other by Tomie dePaola. New York: Putnam Juvenile, 2005. (An excellent book to read before a trip to help senior citizens.) P

Random Acts of Kindness by Conari Press, editors. Berkeley, CA: Conari Press, 2002. (Stories to inspire action.) E/M/T

Sam and the Lucky Money by Karen Chinn. New York: Lee and Low, 1997. (A Chinese custom finds its way to America where a child uses birthday money to help a homeless person.) P

Tell Me a Mitzvah: Little and Big Ways to Repair the World by Danny Siegel. Rockville, MD: Kar-Ben Publishing, 1993. (Stories about people participating in a collection of Jewish philanthropies. The book also includes suggestions about what children can do to help.) E/M/T

Books About Environmental Issues

50 Simple Things Kids Can Do to Save the Earth by The Earthworks Group. Riverside, NJ: Andrews McMeel Publishing, 1990. (Not a storybook, this resource presents the rationale for conservation and provides ideas for projects.) E

City Green by DyAnne DeSalvo-Ryan. New York: Harper Collins, 1994. (Urban cleanup is the theme for this story. It includes instructions for starting a community garden.) P

Fernando's Gift by Douglas Keister. San Francisco: Sierra Club Books for Kids, 2001. (Helps children to realize that when a tree is cut down, it should be replaced with a new tree.) P

The Great Kapok Tree: A Tale of the Amazon Rain Forest by Lynne Cherry. New York: Harcourt, 1990. (If you have children who want to start a "Save the Rainforest" campaign, this is a beautiful book to use.) E

Kid Heroes of the Environment by Katherine Dee. Ashland, OR: Bathroom Readers Press, 1991. (Stories about kids helping the environment.) M

Nora's Duck by Satomi Ichikawa. New York: Philomel Books, 1991. (Use this book to springboard a discussion about the humane treatment of animals by treating and releasing them back to their habitat.) P

Someday a Tree by Eve Bunting. New York: Clarion, 1996. (A good choice to springboard an environmental effort.) E

Something Beautiful by Sharon Dennis Wyeth. Cleveland, OH: Dragonfly Books, 2002. (Look for the beauty even in a trashed urban environment.) E

The Tin Forest by Helene Ward. New York: Dutton, 2001. (Use this book to jump-start a discussion on how to create something beautiful from something unsightly.) P

The Wartville Wizard by Don Madden. New York: Aladdin, 1993. (If you participate in an Adopt-A-Road program, this book will provide the support you need to get kids to participate.) P

Books with the Message to Never Give Up

The Carrot Seed by Ruth Kraus. New York: HarperTrophy, 2004. (When your children lose faith that their project will be successful, read this book.) P

Ducks Disappearing by Phyllis Naylor. New York: Atheneum, 1997. (When a young boy sees ducklings falling into a storm drain, he tries many different ways to get adults to help.) P

Kids with Courage: True Stories About Young People Making a Difference by Barbara A. Lewis. Minneapolis, MN: Free Spirit Publishing, 1992. (Stories of kids who experienced some form of hardship while doing their service projects.) M/T

Books About Small Efforts That Bring Big Accomplishments

The Lady in the Box by Ann McGovern. New York: Turtle Books, 1997. (What to do? Listen to Mom about not talking to strangers or help the homeless lady?) P

The Lion and the Mouse by Gail Herman. New York: Random House Books for Young Readers, 1998. (This Aesop's fable may be used to show children how one small effort can achieve a great and wonderful end.) P

The Little Engine That Could by Watty Piper. New York: Grosset and Dunlap, 1978. (This time-honored tale of a little train is a great way to show that little people can do things that bigger people may not be willing to do.) P

Ordinary Mary's Extraordinary Deed by Emily Pearson. Layton, UT: Gibbs Smith, 2002. (Yes, an ordinary person can make a difference.) P

Pay It Forward by Catherine Ryan Hyde. New York: Pocket Books, 2000. (A novel that teaches us to pass along our good deeds.) T

The Rainbow Fish by Marcus Pfister. New York: North-South Books, 1992. (Read this story in a new way—from the point of view of the other fish in the ocean.) P

Raising Yoder's Barn by Jane Yolen. New York: Little, Brown, 2002. (Everyone pitches in to help restore an Amish family's barn.) P

Books About Working Together

The Can-Do Thanksgiving by Marion Hess Pomerance. Morton Grove, IL: Albert Whitman & Company, 1998. (A young girl wonders where her donated can of peas goes.) P

The Quiltmaker's Gift by Jeff Brumeau. New York: Scholastic, 2001. (If your group is making quilts for needy people, start with this tale of compassion.) E

A Rose for Abby by Donna Guthrie. Nashville, TN: Abingdon Press, 1998. (Abby enlists the help of many people in the neighborhood to prepare a meal for the homeless.) P

Stone Soup by Marcia Brown. New York: Aladdin, 1997. (This time-honored story is still effective in its ability to encourage children to work together for the common good.) E

Swimmy by Leo Lionni. Cleveland, OH: Dragonfly Books, 1973. (Many people together can accomplish what one person acting alone cannot.) P

Uncle Willie and the Soup Kitchen by DyAnne DeSalvo-Ryan. New York: HarperTrophy, 1997. (As the name implies, if your group helps the local soup kitchen, read this book first.) P

Videos That Generate Enthusiasm

Barney: Kids for Character Basics. 30 minutes. Barney Home Video—The Lyons Group, 1996. P

Character Builders: Learn More About Sharing and Kindness. 24 minutes. Bridgestone Multimedia, 2002. (A sing-along) P/E

Winnie the Pooh: Helping Others. 45 minutes. Disney Studios, 1999. P

Winnie the Pooh: Working Together. 33 minutes. Disney Studios, 1999. P

The White House Conference on Philanthropy: Gifts to the Future. 14 minutes. National Council for the Humanities. South Carolina ETV, 1999. M/T

Philanthropy Is. 20 minutes. Minnesota Council on Foundations, 2004. T

Resources for Leaders' Reference

Printed Material on General Organization

Brod, Andrew, Ph.D. "Preparation for the World of Work 2002: A Survey of Employers in Guildford County." Office of Business and Economic Research. University of North Carolina at Greensboro, November 13, 2002.

Brudney, Jeffrey L., Ph.D. and Robert Smariga. Report on the State of Volunteer Centers in 2003, Based on the 2004 Volunteer Center Survey. DC: Points of Light Foundation, 2005.

Johnson, Dorothy A. "Teach Our Children Well." *For the Common Ground.* Vol. 1, No. 1. Fall, 1999.

Marzolo, Jean. *Helping Hands Handbook.* New York: Random House, 1992.

McKee, Jonathan. *Top Ten Resources Youth Leaders Want.* Available from the Source for Youth Ministry, 8863 Greenback Lane –333, Orangevale, CA 95662.

Roberts, Pamela and Alice Yang. *Kids Taking Action: Community Service Learning Projects, K-8.* Turner's Falls, MA: Northeast Foundation for Children, 2002.

Rogers, Fred. *The Giving Box: Create a Tradition of Giving with Your Children.* Philadelphia: Running Press, 2000.

Spaide, Deborah. *Teaching Your Kids to Care.* Bridgewater, NJ: Replica Books, 1999.

Wuthnow, Robert. *Learning to Care: Elementary Kindness in an Age of Indifference.* London: Oxford University Press, 1995.

General Organization Web Sites

www.emu.edu/lillyproject/clc-careers.html
A listing of Web sites that offer careers in service.

www.learningtogive.org
A Web site devoted to educating youth about philanthropy. Check the orders link to purchase books and lesson plans.

www.thesource4ym.com
The Source for Youth Ministry Web site.

http://philanthropy.com
This Web site publishes the Chronicle of Philanthropy online.

www.energizeinc.com/prof.html
Energize, Inc.: This is a resource Web site for leaders of volunteers.

www.afpnet.org
Click on the Youth in Philanthropy link for valuable resources.

http://depts.washington.edu/ccph/pdf_files/slresources-aacp.pdf

National resources for service learning and community campus partner-
ships—a list of Web sites.

www.learningtogive.org/doc/how2guide.doc
A document about the importance of reflection on charitable projects by
young people.

Printed Material About Projects

Kaye, Cathryn Berger. *The Complete Guide to Service Learning: Proven, Practical Ways to Engage Students in Civic Responsibility, Academic Curriculum, and Social Action*. Minneapolis, MN: Free Spirit Publishing, 2003.

Lewis, Barbara A. and Pamela Espeland. *Kid's Guide to Service Projects: Over
500 Service Learning Ideas for Young People Who Want to Make a Difference*. Minneapolis, MN: Free Spirit Publishing, 1995.

Lingo, Susan L. *101 Simple Service Projects Kids Can Do*. Cincinnati, OH:
Standard Publishing Company, 2000.

Web Sites

Projects on Web Sites

www.fiu.edu/~time4chg/Library/ideas.html
This Web site is organized by subject matter and gives ideas for service learning in each. Although it is for college level, ideas may be adapted for
high school students.

www.volunteermatch.org
Insert your zip code and find volunteer opportunities in your area.

www.childrentochildren.org

Children to Children Web site to give duffel bags and stuffed animals to children in foster care.

http://angelsoft.com/angelsinaction/winners/
Stories of kids' award-winning projects.

www.funattic.com/game_youthgroup.htm
Youth group games and ideas for projects.

www.souperbowl.org
A Web site for the Souper Bowl of Caring effort.

Web Sites on Fundraising

www.urban.org/UploadedPDF/411118_foundation_effectiveness.pdf
A research paper discussing the evaluation of a foundation's effectiveness.

www.catholicyouth.org/fundraisers.htm
CYO Web site for some interesting fundraisers.

www.fundraiserhelp.com
Web site offers advice for successful fundraising events.

www.connectforkids.org/node/245
A toolkit for funding with grants.

www.fundraisingweb.org
Which companies provide fundraising schemes in your area? Check at this Web site, which is organized by state, province, and product.

http://fdncenter.org/
The Foundation Center gives regional seminars on grant writing and lists current grants.

www.crisis.org.uk/fund/sleepover.php
A British Web site that offers guidelines for organizing a sleep-a-thon fundraiser.

www.artistshelpingchildren.org/articlecharityparty.html
Guidelines for holding a charitable birthday party for your children to enjoy while earning money for a philanthropy.

www.paservicelearning.org/Resources/Grants/Youth.htm
Pennsylvania grants for youth projects.

www.whitehouse.gov/government/fbci/guidance
Information on U.S. government grants.

www.youthactionnet.org
Information on grants for service projects.

Web Sites About Awards Programs

www.angelsoft.com/angelsinaction
The Angel Soft Angels in Action project recognizes outstanding philanthropic efforts by kids ages 8–18.

www.ysa.org/awards/award_grant.cfm
A listing of awards and grants directly related to Youth Service Day, held the third week in April each year.

www.dosomething.org
Stories of young people changing their world. Click to the awards section for some outstanding projects.

http://startsomething.target.com
Scholarships for youth involved in service projects.

www.prudential.com/overview
Prudential Spirit of Community Award for middle level and high school students doing service projects.

http://pointsoflight.org
National Points of Light Foundation offers awards to people of all ages.

Note: There are also many, many local awards for youth doing philanthropy. Check your local newspapers and Web sites for information.

Index